DISCARDED

The Role of Labor in
African Nation-Building

PRAEGER SPECIAL STUDIES IN
INTERNATIONAL ECONOMICS AND DEVELOPMENT

The Role of Labor in African Nation-Building

Edited by
Willard A. Beling

Proceedings of the Institute
of World Affairs, Volume XLI

FREDERICK A. PRAEGER, Publishers
New York · Washington · London

The purpose of the Praeger Special Studies is to make specialized research monographs in U.S. and international economics and politics available to the academic, business, and government communities. For further information, write to the Special Projects Division, Frederick A. Praeger, Publishers, 111 Fourth Avenue, New York, N.Y. 10003.

FREDERICK A. PRAEGER, PUBLISHERS
111 Fourth Avenue, New York, N.Y. 10003, U.S.A.
77-79 Charlotte Street, London W.1, England

Published in the United States of America in 1968
by Frederick A. Praeger, Inc., Publishers

All rights reserved

© 1968 by Frederick A. Praeger, Inc.

Library of Congress Catalog Card Number: 67-25239

Printed in the United States of America

TO JANNA AND KRISTEN

ACKNOWLEDGMENT

This book grew out of the Forty-Second Session of the Institute of World Affairs, sponsored by the University of Southern California in cooperation with the colleges and universities of the Pacific area.

Organized by the Middle East and North African Program of the University of Southern California's School of International Relations, the conference on *The Role of Labor in Nation-Building* was convened December 5-7, 1965, at the University's mountain campus in Idyllwild, California.

Without the endorsement of the Institute of World Affairs and the sponsorship of the University of Southern California, of course, neither the conference nor this book would have been possible.

W. A. B.

PREFACE

Attracting considerable attention during the national struggles for independence, several African labor leaders became well known internationally. Thus Tom Mboya and Ferhat Hached, to mention only two, were perhaps best known as African nationalists, although in reality they were primarily African labor leaders involved in the nationalist movement. Deriving out of this association, the American labor movement, among others, offered sympathy as well as considerable direct aid during this period to the African nationalist movements.

Tunisian President Habib Bourguiba expressed the gratitude perhaps of most newly independent African states for this support when he addressed the Fifth World Congress of the International Confederation of Free Trade Unions (ICFTU) which was held, significantly, in Africa in July, 1957:

> It is a pleasure to recall here the outstanding services rendered by the Tunisian trade union movement to the cause of the liberation of Tunisia, as well as the considerable contribution which the ICFTU made to that cause....[1]

With this as a background, therefore, many naturally

---

[1] ICFTU, *Report of the Fifth World Congress, Held in Tunis 5-13 July 1957* (Brussels: 1957), p. 231 ff. See also Willard A. Beling, *Modernization and African Labor: A Tunisian Case Study* (New York: Praeger, 1965), pp. 40-57 and 81-99.

expected the African labor movements also to play a commensurately important role in the postindependence period. The African labor movements failed, however, to measure up to expectations and thus disappointed a number of their non-African supporters.

This book examines African labor's role within the post-independence period or, as political scientists are wont to term it, the nation-building period. With one exception, the chapters are derived from papers presented at the conference on *The Role of Labor in Nation-Building* which the Institute of World Affairs, under the sponsorship of the University of Southern California, convened December 5-7, 1965, in Idyllwild, California.

The papers passed under the close scrutiny of a number of trade unionists and scholars, as well as representatives from the U.S. Departments of Labor and State, who attended the conference. Such people provided a realistic backdrop which academic conferences sometimes lack. Hopefully, the vitality that they brought to the conference is reflected in the revised papers presented in this book.

The following African labor leaders participated in the conference:

    Alhaji Adebola, Nigerian United Labor Congress
    Mahjoub Ben Seddik, *Union Marocaine du Travail*
    René Delanne, *Union Nationale des Travailleurs du Niger*
    Kotshoe Dube, Zimbabwe African Peoples Union (Rhodesia)
    Malik Fall, *Union des Travailleurs de Mauritanie*
    G. B. Fogam, National Union of Plantation and Industrial Workers of the Cameroon
    Alphonse R. Kithima, *Confédération des Syndicats Libres du Congo*
    Nana Mahomo, South African exile, Editor of *Crisis and Change*
    Doudou N'Gom, *Union Nationale des Travailleurs du Sénégal*
    George Palmer, Sierra Leone Federation of Labor
    Ahmed Tlili, former General Secretary, *Union Générale Tunisienne du Travail*

Fulton Yancy, Liberian Congress of Industrial Organizations

The following professors from various universities and colleges of the Pacific area participated formally as discussants on the various papers presented at the conference: Charles F. Andrain, Arthur Carstens, Kenneth W. Grundy, Aurelius Morgner, Charles R. Nixon, Georges Sabagh and George O. Totten. Other formal discussants with a specialized knowledge in the field of international labor were Frank Ferrari, Corning Glass International; William Steen, U.S. Department of Labor; and Giles Wright, II, of the Fund for International Social and Economic Education. Arnold Beichman, international correspondent and writer; Irving Brown, Executive Director, African-American Labor Center, and ICFTU representative to the United Nations; and George P. Delaney, U.S. Department of State, chaired various sessions of the conference.

As Executive Director of the African-American Labor Center, Irving Brown was instrumental in bringing all the African leaders, with the exception of Mahjoub Ben Seddik, to the conference. Out of keen interest in examining the role of labor in nation-building, he diverted the group of African labor leaders from their itinerary to participate in this academic discussion. They were en route to the AFL-CIO Convention which was scheduled to convene in San Francisco shortly after the Idyllwild conference. The others came as guests of the Institute of World Affairs.

The editor wishes to thank the various authors for their contributions to the volume which, it is interesting to observe, displays unusual consensus. This is all the more remarkable, since the contributors were invited from a broad spectrum of disciplines and backgrounds, both academic and governmental. The views and opinions expressed by the authors from the Departments of Labor and State, of course, are those of the authors and should in no way be interpreted as reflecting official policy of their respective departments or of the U.S. Government.

Finally, the editor takes the opportunity to acknowledge the work of the staff of the Middle East/North African Program of the University of Southern California in convening the conference and preparing the manuscript which derived from it.

Woodland Hills, California   W. A. B.

CONTENTS

	Page
ACKNOWLEDGMENT	vii
PREFACE	ix
LIST OF TABLES	xvii
ABBREVIATIONS	xix

PART I THE POLITICAL ROLE OF LABOR IN NATION-BUILDING

Chapter

1 THE POLITICAL STATUS OF AFRICAN TRADE UNIONS
Michael F. Lofchie and Carl G. Rosberg, Jr.   3

The Primacy of Economic Development	6
The Need to Stabilize Political Authority	8
The Multifunctional Role of African Trade Unions	9
Relative Autonomy	10
Semicontrolled Situations	11
Controlled Unions	12
Prevailing Elite Values	13
Conclusion	18

2 LABOR'S ROLE IN EMERGING AFRICAN SOCIALIST STATES
William H. Friedland   20

Government's Projected Role for the Unions	21
Disciplining for Productivity	23
Capital Accumulation	26
Administering Social Services	28
Union Response to Governmental Programs	30

Chapter	Page
Disciplining for Productivity	31
Capital Accumulation	34
Administering Social Services	35
The Unions' Self-Image	36

PART II THE ECONOMIC ROLE OF LABOR IN NATION-BUILDING

3 LABOR DEVELOPMENT AND ECONOMIC MODERNIZATION
Everett M. Kassalow   41

Labor Force Recruitment and Commitment: The Setting for Labor Development	42
Migratory Labor Hinders African Labor Development	43
Reasons for Varying Area Patterns of Commitment	47
The Attraction of City Life: The Other Side of Migration	51
Africa: The Racial Factors in Labor Development	54
Race and Wage Differentials	57
Trade Unionism and Modernization	58
Unions Committed to Modernization Process	59
Trade Unionism and Economic Development	61
Economic Planning and Unionism in the Developing Countries	63
Wage Policies in the New Countries	64
Unionism and the Problems of Inflation and Equity in Development	66
Trade Unions and Social Overhead Investment	70
Union Participation in Other Nation-Building Activities	70

4 URBANIZATION AND THE LABOR FORCE
Alvin H. Scaff   73

African Urbanization in Perspective	75
The African Social Structure and Labor	79
Conclusion	93

Chapter	Page

5 THE DEVELOPMENT OF TRADE UNIONS IN NEW NATIONS
Arnold M. Zack   95

Labor's Postindependence Period	95
The Question of Trade Union Autonomy	97
Alternative Union Programs in New Nations	97
Participation in National Planning	98
Skill Development	98
Cooperatives, Housing and Health Programs	99
Implementing Alternative Programs	100
Conclusion	102

6 NATION-BUILDING AND THE INTERNATIONAL FREE TRADE UNION MOVEMENT
Daniel C. Lazorchick and Charles R. Hare   103

Government Attitudes Toward Trade Unions	105
African Trade Union Functions	107
Processing Worker Grievances	107
Bargaining in the Private Sector	108
Providing Social Services	110
International Trade Union Involvement	112
International Trade Union Assistance	115
The Challenge	116

PART III   LABOR'S ROLE IN SUPRANATION-BUILDING

7 LABOR: STUMBLING BLOCK TO PAN-AFRICANISM
Dorothy Nelkin   121

The Continental Trade Union Organizations	122
The All African Trade Union Federation	123
The African Regional Organization	124
The African Trade Union Confederation	126
The Affiliation Issue	127
The Need of External Support	127
The Availability of External Support	128
The Histadrut	130
African-American Labor Center	130
External Support from the East	131
The International Impact on Pan-Africanism	131
The National Orientation of Labor	132

Chapter		Page
	Role of Unions in National Development	133
	Political Orientation of Labor	135
	Diversity in Union Power	135
	Conclusion	137
8	AFRICAN TRADE UNIONS AND THE COLD WAR George E. Lichtblau	139
	States and Unions in Alliance	140
	The Internationals and the Independence Struggle	143
	The Internationals in the British Colonies	144
	The Internationals in the French Colonies	147
	ICFTU Regionalism and the Pan-African Labor Movement	154
	The Confrontation in Africa	156
	Internationalism and Internal Conflicts	158
	The Communists and the Pan-African Labor Movement	162
	Ghana and the AATUF	167
	Conclusion	169
9	EURAFRICANISM: IMPACT ON AFRICAN LABOR Willard A. Beling	171
	Eurafricanism	173
	Seeds of Conflict in Eurafricanism	176
	Europe: Primus Inter Pares	177
	Eurafricanism: Equated with Neocolonialism	180
	Europe: Meeting the Challenge?	183
	Pan-African Frustrations and Failures	186
	Viable Alternatives to Eurafricanism?	191
	Relations Outside the Eurafrican Framework	193
	Conclusion	195
10	LABOR: THE PROBLEM OF INTERNATIONAL DIALOGUE Donald C. Bergus	197
	The Dialogue within the Atlantic Community	198
	The Dialogue with the Developing Areas	198
	Ideological Factors	200
	Sociological and Economic Factors	201
	Political Factors	203
	Conclusion	204

LIST OF TABLES

Table		Page
1	Population Density: Africa, Asia, and Latin America	47
2	Trend in Ratio of Money Income per Person Engaged in Manufacturing to that per Person Engaged in Agriculture	68
3	Level of Urbanization in Selected African States	76
4	Percentage of Households by Number of Persons in Each Household, Kisenyi, 1964 Compared with 1954	82
5	Distribution of Kisenyi Population by Age Groups	83
6	School Attendance in Kisenyi and All Uganda	84
7	Marital Distribution of Kisenyi Adult Males in 1964	84
8	Kisenyi Plural Marriages by Religious Faith	85
9	Distribution of Kisenyi Property Owners by Origin	86
10	Distribution of Kisenyi Inhabitants by Length of Residence	87

Table		Page
11	Rentals in Kisenyi in 1954 and 1964	89
12	Occupations, All Adults 16 and Over, Kisenyi, 1964	90
13	Number of Customary Holdings in Four Kibuya Parishes, by Distance from Kampala's Western Boundary: 1938 and 1956	92
14	Average Size of Customary Holding in Four Kibuya Parishes, by Distance from Kampala's Western Boundary, 1957	92
15	Comparison of African ICFTU Affiliates in 1962 and 1964	125
16	Exports of Selected African States	187

ABBREVIATIONS

AALC	African-American Labor Center
AATUC	All Africa Trade Union Confederation
AATUF	All Africa Trade Union Federation
ACFTU	All China Federation of Trade Unions
AFL-CIO	American Federation of Labor-Congress of Industrial Organizations
AFRO	African Regional Organization (of the ICFTU)
ARO	Asian Regional Organization (of the ICFTU)
AUCCTU	All Union Central Council of Trade Unions
BDS	Bloc Démocratique Sénégalais (of Senegal)
CAWU	Commercial and Allied Workers Union
CFDT	Confédération Française Démocratique du Travail
CGT	Confédération Générale du Travail (of France)
CGTA	Confédération Générale des Travailleurs d'Afrique
CISC	International Federation of Christian Trade Unions
COTU	Central Organization of Trade Unions (of Kenya)
EACSO	East African Common Service Organization
EEC	European Economic Community
EFTA	European Free Trade Association
FDGB	West German Trade Union Federation
FGTB	Belgian General Federation of Labor
FLN	National Liberation Front (of Algeria)
FUTU	Federation of Uganda Trade Unions
GATT	General Agreement on Tariffs and Trade
CGT-FO	Confédération Générale du Travail-Force Ouvrière (of France)
GTUC	Ghana Trade Union Congress
ICATU	International Confederation of Arab Trade Unions
ICFTU	International Confederation of Free Trade Unions
IFCTU	International Federation of Christian Trade Unions
ILO	International Labor Organization (or Office)

IMF	International Miners Federation
ITF	International Transportation Workers Federation
ITS	International Trade Secretariats
MCF	Movement for Colonial Freedom
MRP	Mouvement de Rassemblement Populaire
NUTA	National Union of Tanganyikan Workers
OAU	Organization of African Unity
OCAM	Organisation Commune Africaine et Malgache
OEEC	Organization for European Economic Cooperation
OGB	Austrian Trade Union Federation
ORIT	Inter-American Regional Organization (ICFTU)
PCF	Parti Communiste Français (of France)
RDA	Rassemblement Démocratique Africain
SFIO	Section Française de l'Internationale Ouvrière (French Socialist Party)
TANU	Tanganyika African National Union
TFL	Tanganyikan Federation of Labor
UAM	Union Africaine et Malgache (African francophonic union)
UGTA	Union Générale des Travailleurs Algériens
UGTAN	Union Générale des Travailleurs d'Afrique Noire
UGTT	Union Générale Tunisienne du Travail
UMT	Union Marocaine du Travail
UNIP	United National Independence Party
UPIC	Pan-African Union of Believing Workers
USTA	United Trade Union Federation of Algerian Labor
WFTU	World Federation of Trade Unions
WIC	Workers Investment Corporation
ZTUC	Zambian Trade Union Congress

PART I

THE POLITICAL ROLE OF
LABOR IN NATION-BUILDING

CHAPTER 1 THE POLITICAL STATUS OF
AFRICAN TRADE UNIONS

Michael F. Lofchie and Carl G. Rosberg, Jr.[†]

The achievement of independence has created a crisis in government-trade union relations in Africa. The major ingredients in this crisis are a belief among African political leaders that unions must now relate themselves to the problems of creating new national societies and the assumption that the national governments will determine what form this relationship must assume. The problem arises out of the fact that effective union participation in the process of nation-building requires a more clearly prescribed role for the unions and far closer ties and cooperation between union and political leadership than was present during the era of nationalism. Thus, one of the most striking trends in Africa today is the effort by newly established governments to institutionalize firm controls over trade union movements. In many cases, such as Ghana, Guinea and Tanzania, this is part of a broad political effort to establish state supervision and management of a wide array of conventionally autonomous institutional structures (e.g., bureaucracies, armies, cooperative movements), while in other countries trade unions are singled out for special attention.

[†]Michael F. Lofchie is Assistant Professor of Political Science, University of California, Los Angeles, and the author of *Zanzibar: Background to Revolution* (1965) and a number of articles on Africa. Carl G. Rosberg, Jr., is Associate Professor of Political Science and Chairman of the Committee for African Studies of the Institute of International Studies, University of California, Berkeley. He is the author of *Africa and the World Today* (1966); co-editor of the *Kenyatta Elections: Kenya 1960-1961* (1961); co-editor of *African Socialism* (1964) and of *Political Parties and National Integration in Tropical Africa* (1964). [Although they make some references to the labor movements of North Africa, the authors confine their remarks for the most part to sub-Saharan Africa.--Editor.]

The subordination of trade union movements to state control is in marked contrast to the late colonial period when, generally speaking, trade unions enjoyed a high degree of autonomy from African political movements. Nationalism did not demand that unions define their relationship to politics in a precise way. The ideology of nationalism was highly diffuse, and any sort of opposition to colonial rule constituted an acceptable and important contribution to the struggle for independence. Since the goal of nationalism was to undermine the legitimacy and authority of alien European rule, unions were able to render valuable assistance to nationalism merely by sharing and articulating the anticolonial values of the nationalist movements. There was no need and only limited expectation that they play a greater role. Thus, the widespread generalization that trade unions formed an integral component of African nationalist movements is, as Elliott Berg and Jeffrey Butler have pointed out,[1] largely erroneous. In the preindependence era, trade unions exhibited their fundamental independence from nationalist leadership in several different ways. Many African trade unions were relatively nonpolitical and, aside from a general sympathy for the goals of nationalism, took only limited interest in the politics of independence. An example of this situation is Ghana, where the efforts of nationalist leaders to generate increased political consciousness and activity among trade unionists led to considerable friction between the Convention People's Party and the Ghana Trade Union Congress. Even where trade unions demonstrated high political awareness, for example French Cameroon, this was not necessarily accompanied by a relationship of cooperation and agreement between the unions and the nationalist political parties.

The historic autonomy of trade unions during the colonial era casts serious doubt on the assumption that common opposition to European rule fomented strong and early bonds between union leadership and nationalist politicians. It is probably more accurate to interpret colonial rule as an important factor in accounting for union separatism. Britain, France and Belgium brought to Africa a set of Western atti-

---

[1] See Elliott Berg and Jeffrey Butler, "Trade Unions" in James Coleman and Carl Rosberg (eds.), *Political Parties and National Integration in Tropical Africa* (Berkeley: University of California Press, 1964), pp. 340-381.

tudes toward the appropriate role and status of trade unions. The most important operative component of these was a notion of social pluralism, the concept that unions are to be viewed as private interest groups, and that their appropriate role is to seek to maximize the social and economic advantages of their own membership. In this vision of society, trade unions were simply one segment of a heterogeneous assortment of voluntary associations competing against one another for the attainment of primarily economic rather than political goals. Colonial governments possessed numerous techniques to bring about this sort of trade unionism within the African setting. They could, for example, encourage unionists to believe that if they avoided sensitive political issues, they would escape the repressions and restrictions imposed on nationalist movements. Or, if necessary, colonial powers could use direct legislative and administrative techniques to sever incipient ties between the unions and the nationalist parties.

Western labor movements also played an important part, during the colonial period, in fostering an early tradition of "free" trade unionism in Africa. Such groups as the International Confederation of Free Trade Unions (ICFTU), the General Confederation of Workers (CGT) and the International Federation of Christian Trade Unions (IFCTU) provided critical organizational and financial assistance in many countries during the formative period of African trade unions, and the close personal and organizational ties between African unionists and their Western counterparts contributed significantly to the emergence of an attitude of autonomous trade unionism. Thus, the present tendency toward close integration of union movements with dominant political parties and state institutions cannot be viewed simply as the continuation of an institutional pattern established during the colonial period. Rather, it represents a response to the special conditions and problems associated with independence.

At least three aspects of the postcolonial situation may be singled out as relevant to an explanation of why African governments have sought to control and discipline the trade union movements within their societies. These are the primacy of economic development, the need to consolidate and stabilize political authority, and the differing role trade unions are expected to play in the postindependence setting.

THE PRIMACY OF ECONOMIC DEVELOPMENT

African leaders view economic development as their primary objective, and, in Africa, the inducement of economic change is an overwhelmingly political task. Unlike Western industrial societies where economic development was a product of the activities of a private entrepreneurial class, African societies must depend upon state leadership and initiative in the effort to bring about rapid social and economic change. Generally lacking in substantial numbers of investment-oriented entrepreneurs, African nations must rely for their economic dynamism upon massive politico-administrative efforts in the creation and implementation of centralized development plans. Central planning is, in effect, a functional substitute for private capitalism. If it is to be effective, however, development through central planning necessitates a high degree of governmental control over major sectors of the economy, including such factors as wages and, to a large extent, labor conduct. Unanticipated wage increases or sporadic strikes can upset the balance of a comprehensive development plan and critically jeopardize its chances of success. Moreover, African leaders are confronted with a critical lack of the necessary physical, economic and infrastructural prerequisites for development, and therefore consider it indispensable to mobilize the human and organizational resources of their societies. As a result of all these factors, control over trade unions has come to be viewed as a major imperative of almost any sort of state-administered economic development.

There is a second major difference between the historic process of development which occurred in the West and that are presently occurring in Africa. In Western societies, Great Britain for example, industrialization was more or less completed long before the establishment of organized trade unionism. Workers as a group were not in a position to challenge prevailing wages or conditions of work, and the capacity of the early industrial system to pass successfully through the initial stages of capital accumulation probably depended in some measure upon its ability to impose harsh and regimented conditions upon the working class. Organized trade unions oriented toward higher wages and improved conditions of work emerged only after the industrial process had become an ongoing phenomenon and was able to sustain workers' economic demands. In Africa, relatively well-organized trade unions have come into existence at the earliest phase of economic development, and their tendency is to make demands upon the system quite comparable to those made by Western unions at a more mature period of industrialization. As a result, African leaders have frequently come to feel that while it may not be necessary for African workers to endure the same degree of deprivation that accompanied the Western Industrial Revolution, it may well be essential for them to accept some austerity and sacrifice if the broad public interest in development is to be served.

The widespread belief among African leaders that the public interest may be precisely defined in terms of the absolute necessity for economic development is, in and of itself, relevant to the gradual creation of administrative and legal mechanisms for the regulation of trade unions. For the ethos of development does not furnish a basic principle of legitimacy guaranteeing the right of private groups to engage in self-interested activities, and thus constitutes a restrictive standard of group conduct. To underline this point, it may be useful to contrast the ethos of development with the historic concept of "public interest" in the Western political tradition. In classical liberal political theory, the public interest tended to be viewed in pluralistic terms as the clash of competitive interest groups, each seeking to maximize its own advantage. In this view, the role of government is limited to the protection of individual's life and property.

As the Western concept of public interest has shifted to construe the role of government in more positive and activist terms, this change has been accompanied by increasing regulation of labor, business and other private interests. Indeed, restrictions on labor freedom in the public sector and in critical social services such as transportation have long been common in the United States. The contemporary notion that governmental supervision rather than a network of competitive voluntary associations constitutes the basic defense of the public interest exactly parallels the African emphasis on economic development. In both, the socially acceptable range of group conduct is limited by the state on the basis that maximum group freedom is not intrinsically compatible with the public good.

THE NEED TO STABILIZE POLITICAL AUTHORITY

A compelling motive behind the effort to control trade unions is the need, in many African countries, to consolidate and stabilize political authority. Once having achieved independence, African regimes face serious problems of organizational weakness, limited penetration of society by political structures and the fragility of formal institutions. These problems have prompted African leaders to seek and employ novel approaches in order to increase the viability of their political systems and in order to ensure a minimum degree of social control. One such method is the incorporation of conventionally autonomous, potentially dissident social groups into the state structure or dominant party. In positive terms, the integration of such groups, trade unions included, is viewed as a principal method of enhancing the developmental capability of the national political system.

One of the major factors of institutional weakness in many African states is the vulnerability of dominant political elites. In part, this can be attributed to a striking cultural gap between elite and mass. For the most part, African elites are strongly oriented toward Western attitudes, norms and styles of life, even where their ideological sympathies lie elsewhere. The vast majority of Africans, however, remain rooted in a traditional setting, both geographically and emotionally. This cultural gap creates a natural tendency for the elite to become politically alienated from the mass of the population. Moreover, the cultural gap is often accompanied by visible differences in income and style of life. African elites enjoy many of the social and economic amenities of advanced industrial countries, whereas the mass of the population continues to dwell in the comparatively impoverished circumstances of rural agrarian societies. The relative deprivation of the mass increases with the affluence of the elite. Radical cultural and economic differentiation along these lines weakens the legitimacy of the elite and renders it open to social criticism from below.

The elite-mass gap has a special bearing on the political status of trade unions in Africa. On the one hand, trade unions can function as a middle group between elite and mass and, by their support of the regime, help to bridge the gap. On the other hand, trade union leadership is perhaps best situated to take advantage of the extreme social distance which characterizes elite-mass relations. Union leaders have a firm organizational basis within the trade union movements and are, as a rule, far closer to the mass of the people socio-economically. Since union leadership does not bear direct responsibility for economic development, it is in a position to criticize inadequacies or failures in the development process. It can thus capitalize on the "rising expectations" of the broad mass of the population and place itself in the position of championing the aspirations of the entire people, not merely union membership. Moreover, unions tend to occupy a politically strategic position in the society; their greatest strength is in the large cities and in those sectors of the economy which are vital to modernization--mining, transportation, commercial agriculture and social services. For all these reasons, African trade unions possess an enormous political potential.[2] Indeed, aside from the dominant political parties themselves, unions probably constitute the strongest political force in a large number of African states. The unions' potential, either in helping shape a strong consensus or in exploiting the possibility of elite-mass alienation, helps explain why African political leaders are eager to establish firm controls over union organizations and leaders.

THE MULTIFUNCTIONAL ROLE OF AFRICAN TRADE UNIONS

African unions must perform a substantially different and more varied role than their Western counterparts. This view is widely held and frequently articulated by African political leaders. Their argument tends to run along the following lines: As opposed to Western unions, which perform an almost exclusively "consumptionist" function, seeking improved wages, benefits and working conditions for their own members, African unions, if they are to be effectively involved in nation-building, must play a broad "productionist" role. That is, they bear a major responsibility for increasing over-all economic output while accepting conditions of austerity, so that the entire society may benefit. In addition, African unions must perform a variety of novel functions stemming from the transitional state of their societies. They must, for example, act as agencies of sociali-

---

[2]The authors are indebted to Professor William Friedland for this idea and for his other valuable comments.

zation introducing traditional agrarian populations to the rhythms, patterns and behavioral codes of industrial life. They must act as educational institutions, training unfamiliar workers in the managerial and technical skills socially necessary for development.

The unions' responsibilities as socializing and educative mechanisms extend as well into the political realm; they must convey the importance of a sense of national citizenship and involvement and attempt to erode regional and parochial loyalties. In addition, unions must work actively to support other social institutions involved in the process of nation-building, such as national cooperative movements or local self-help schemes. All these views perceive the trade unions as an integral feature of the government's efforts toward nation-building and economic development and may help explain why political leaders are anxious to discipline and manage their labor movements.

Although the trend toward a consolidation of political power over trade unions is a universal theme in virtually all independent African states, there is wide variation in actual experience. The African countries differ considerably in the actual degree of control they have established over their trade unions and even in the extent to which they have sought to do so. Many African trade unions remain relatively free of political supervision and can practice a style of union activity directly reminiscent of the AFL-CIO or the TUC. At the opposite extreme are those African unions which have been so fully integrated into the political system that they are virtually indistinguishable from the state itself. Within this enormous range of variation, it may be useful to distinguish three broad categories: relative autonomy, semicontrolled situations, and full governmental control.

RELATIVE AUTONOMY

The concept of "relative autonomy" is intended to describe those African countries where trade unions have retained a fairly high degree of associational freedom. Perhaps the best examples of this situation are Nigeria, Sierra Leone, Mauritania, Morocco and Congo (Leopoldville). In these countries the activities and orientation of the trade union movements cortion of the trade union movements into the administration, the dominant party, or both. Examples of this situation are Ghana, Mali, Guinea and Tanzania. Here, administrative integration has enabled national political leadership to exercise full managerial and policy control over the unions. In these countries, managerial and policy controls are supplemented by a range of legislation affecting such labor activities as the right to strike and the internal conduct of union affairs.

Tanzania furnishes an excellent example of a "controlled" situation. A wholly new trade union movement, the National Union of Tanganyika Workers (NUTA), was established in 1963 and placed under the direct control of the Ministry of Labor. NUTA is closely affilliated to the governing party, the Tanganyika African National Union (TANU), and its representatives sit on the Cabinet and the TANU executive. NUTA is, however, completely controlled by government officials. The President names NUTA's General Secretary and Vice General Secretary and NUTA budgets must be approved by the Ministry of Labor. Without the expressed authorization of the Ministry of Labor, NUTA can spend no more than 40 per cent of its revenue on administration, the balance being earmarked for social projects and services designated by the Ministry of Labor.

This wide range of variation among African states is doubtless the product of a large number of individual circumstances and situations which may differ considerably from country to country. The stability of the government, the state of the economy, the nature of the party system and the internal characteristics of the unions themselves, for example, are but a few of the many considerations which affect the character of relations between political leadership and trade unions. Of all the factors which may bear upon the extent to which political leadership actively seeks and successfully establishes dominance over trade unions, two may be singled out as having special importance. These are the politico-economic values of the dominant elite and internal societal considerations.

PREVAILING ELITE VALUES

The politico-economic values of the dominant elite have

enormous bearing on the status of trade unions. Clearly, the political motivation to move rapidly and decisively to control the unions is far greater in those states where political leaders have a commitment to a *dirigiste* or state-managed economy. Indeed, subordination of unions to political discipline seems implicit in the very concept of economic collectivism. On the other hand, where elite values tend to stress a higher degree of economic permissiveness and tolerance for an admixture of free enterprise and statism in the economic system, this attitude will probably result in greater union freedom. Varying elite values seem helpful in accounting for the difference between Kenya, a transitional situation, and Ghana, a government-controlled situation. Kenya's present political leadership places great stress on economic pragmatism, and a long-established private economy is viewed as a potentially valuable asset for future growth.

This permissiveness has been reflected in the approach to trade unions. Kenya's leaders have sought flexibility in the degree of control they impose over the unions, avoiding any all-out subordination of the Central Organization of Trade Unions (COTU) to governmental discipline. In Ghana, a strong and widespread belief in the value of a state-directed, collectivized economy has furnished substantial ideological impetus to the establishment of a politically disciplined trade union movement.

It is important to distinguish two separate forms of political permissiveness in contemporary Africa. The first, that exemplified by Kenya, is born of economic liberalism. Union autonomy is the product of a generalized tolerance for social and economic freedom. The second form of permissiveness is of a more conservative sort. In Ethiopia and Liberia, trade unions today enjoy a fairly high degree of autonomy, but here trade union freedom is largely the product of the fundamental concern of the dominant elites to maintain a political status quo. Ethiopian and Liberian leaders are unwilling to integrate trade unions into the state structure, for this might mean surrendering positions of power to social elements unsympathetic to existing political arrangements. Moreover, there is extreme reluctance which might generate social discontent in the modernizing sectors. Another factor which may help protect union autonomy in these two countries is an unwillingness to employ policies of social control which would add further to

(UNIP), which, they felt, had not provided the unions with a fair number of seats in the National Assembly or Cabinet. Some union officials also felt that the government had not done enough to reduce the differential status of European and African workers on the copperbelt where expatriates still enjoyed higher salaries and amenities than Africans. Government officials feared that prolonged strikes, especially on the copperbelt, might cripple the Zambian economy and, in early 1965, passed regulative legislation. The new law recognized only one trade union movement, the Zambia Trade Union Congress (ZTUC), and compelled all other unions in the country to affiliate to it. According to the terms of the law, the government was to appoint ZTUC leadership. Moreover, the ZTUC was forbidden either to affiliate to international bodies without governmental consent or to accept financial assistance from overseas. Perhaps most important, no strike could be held without the consent of the Minister of Labor.

New trade union legislation in Uganda illustrates a somewhat different pattern of semicontrol, one emphasizing greater scrutiny by the government of internal union affairs.[4] A recently passed law gives the Minister for Housing and Labor a vast range of powers over the management, staffing and financial affairs of the Uganda trade unions. He can, for example, call in for inspection all books and documents related to trade union affairs. Failure to comply with this requirement or irregularities in the administration of the unions can lead to prosecution of union officials or cancellation of a union's registration, a virtual death blow since unregistered unions cannot legally exist and employers are forbidden to deal with unions which do not have governmental recognition. Another important power which this law gives the Uganda Government is the right, under certain conditions, to declare top union officials unfit to hold office.

CONTROLLED UNIONS

The concept "controlled unions" is intended to describe those African societies where the effort to bring about political dominance of trade unions has resulted in the full integra-

---

[4]*Reporter* (East Africa), April 25, 1965.

respond somewhat to the classical pluralistic model of the Anglo-American tradition. Two of the chief characteristics of "relative autonomy" are the right to strike and the freedom to choose their leaders. This also implies that internal management and organization of the unions are free of governmental scrutiny.

SEMICONTROLLED SITUATIONS

As the term "semicontrolled" implies, this category is intended to include all those countries where a certain amount of state supervision and control over trade unions has been established but where this control falls short of full integration of the trade union movement into the political system. The principal examples of this situation are Kenya, Uganda, Ivory Coast, Senegal and Zambia. The primary characteristic of the semicontrolled situation is that at least one, and sometimes several, forms of governmental regulation have been employed to limit trade union autonomy. While such controls may take a wide variety of forms, the most frequent are government appointment or selection of trade union leaders, the need for official recognition in order for a union to operate, and the restriction of international affiliation. Of these, the necessity for governmental recognition is particularly important. Since the right to recognize implies the right not to recognize, this measure can be used to introduce subtle and indirect pressures on the internal conduct of trade union affairs.

The Zambian case offers an excellent example of a semicontrolled situation and of the use of a mixture of different forms of governmental regulation in response to a series of problems within the trade union movement and in government-union relations.[3] In brief, by the end of 1964, Zambia's trade unions had become bitterly divided along personal, ideological and, to an extent, tribal lines. Inter- and intra-union conflicts had led to a condition of virtual chaos in the union movement. Many unionists were bitterly critical of the government and the governing party, the United National Independence Party

---

[3]*Central African Examiner*, December, 1964, and May, 1965.

their image as quasi-feudal, autocratic regimes.

Political elites are not free to impose controls on trade unions in accordance with ideological commitments. The nature of the social context within which they operate may extend or limit the degree to which union discipline is politically feasible. Where societies are highly pluralistic in terms of competing political groups, the national authority structure will probably have to accommodate continuing bases of social conflict. More precisely, where ethnic, regional or group loyalties are strong and viable, national leadership must concern itself primarily with maintaining a continuing consensus and strengthening over-all unity; decisions affecting development and economic affairs must be carefully weighed for their impact on the over-all fabric of social integration. Unions may be able to take advantage of this situation to maximize their own autonomy. Only in those societies where the ethnic system is relatively weak, and where politics can be focused on developmental rather than consensual priorities, can there be said to exist a social situation accommodative of union discipline, since the tensions generated by the imposition of controls over trade unions are likely to upset the over-all stability of the government.

Societal considerations of this sort help explain the difference between the status of trade unions in Nigeria (relative autonomy) and Tanzania (government control). In Nigeria, a loose federal system has been necessary to accommodate the divisive and separatist ethnic solidarities within a national political framework; politics is a highly pluralistic and competitive process and political leaders have had to fashion public policy in accordance with a critical need to maintain a consensus. The Nigerian general election in December, 1964, gave all-too-vivid evidence of the extremely delicate balance of factors on which continued federal unity depends. In practical terms, the fragility of the political system has meant that the Nigerian Government has had to adapt itself to highly assertive interests and associational group pressures of all sorts. Trade unions in Nigeria have been able to capitalize on this political contest and function freely and openly in the interests of their membership. However, this may mean that trade union autonomy is less a product of a political commitment to pluralism than an unwilling recognition that interest groups cannot be contained without possibly damaging over-all political unity.

In Tanzania, the ethnic system is relatively weak politically and the government has not had to cope with divisive tribal loyalties. Differential social mobilization has not figured prominently in Tanzanian politics, and no single tribal group or cluster of tribes is sufficiently central to the national political scene to pose a threat to other ethnic communities. A common language (Swahili) has also contributed to national integration. For all these reasons, it has been far easier here, than in Nigeria, for TANU leadership to incorporate trade unions as well as other subgroups (e.g., cooperatives, local government) into the national state structure. There is also a sense in which the absence of highly mobilized ethnic groups has made it more essential to control functional subgroups (civil servants, trade unionists, army). When the army mutiny of January, 1964, occurred, and, after a few days, was supported by a group of dissident trade unionists, there was no solid tribal basis of support which the government could rally to its cause. Tanzania's principal tribes were either too distant from Dar es Salaam or insufficiently mobilized for effective involvement in national politics. Without a core basis of ethnic support, TANU leadership found it necessary to turn to Great Britain for assistance. The army and the unions had posed a far greater threat to the viability of the regime because their presence and assertiveness at the center of national politics were unchecked and unbalanced by other social forces. This factor, too, may help explain why Tanzania's leadership has felt it necessary to bring the army and the trade unions under close state supervision.

The major implicit premise of the argument thus far has been that a situation of latent structural tension exists between political elites and trade unions in Africa. This tension may be explicitly stated in the following terms. In the interests of economic development, national integration, and of having the unions perform a complex multifunctional role, dominant political elites wish to establish firm administrative and policy controls over union organizations. Unions, however, wish insofar as possible to operate autonomously to pursue the maximum economic and social advantages for their members. Although many African states feature cordial and cooperative relations between government and union, a widespread and more frequent incidence of friction would appear to validate the original premise. It is therefore useful, at this point, to conceptualize the relationship as one involving at least potential conflict and to consider the comparative resources and strategies available to each. The utility of this approach is that it furnishes one method of assessing possible future trends in government-union relations.

The conclusion is inescapable that in terms of the resources and strategies for exercising political power, governments possess an overwhelming advantage. They can, if they wish, bring the entire legislative, administrative and coercive power of the state to bear on unions. This furnishes political leadership with an almost inexhaustible list of punishments and rewards. It will suffice to mention only a few of the available techniques of union discipline. Through legislation, it is possible to forbid strikes, to regulate collective bargaining, to establish administration scrutiny over internal union affairs and to demand fiscal accountability. There have been cases in which governments have also used this power to regulate or to cut off unions from international affiliation, an important source of funds. Ultimately, it is possible to resort to direct suppression of union leadership through banishment or rustication. On the reward side, governments can confer on unions the right to establish a check-off system; favor one union against another by conferring or withholding recognition; and provide union leaders with formalized access to political power by reserving cabinet assignments, parliamentary seats or other high positions for union personnel. Informally, the dominant elite can employ its virtual monopoly of status, prestige and material rewards to co-opt individual union leaders into the political establishment.

All this is not to suggest that unions do not possess some important means of preserving autonomy. Unions do possess organization and membership, significant sources of power in any political context. And although the total number of union members may be small in relation to the whole society, the unions operate at the heart of the modernizing sector of the national economy. They have their greatest strength in the towns and in those industries that are economically vital: on the docks, in mining, on the commercial agricultural estates or in the public sector. Their location endows unions with an explosive political potential: A well-organized and effectively conducted strike could easily paralyze a society, as the Nigerian general strike of 1965 illustrated. As a general rule, however, the unions are simply not as well endowed with the resources of power as the state. The sheer magnitude of the resources available to political leadership would seem to suggest that in the foreseeable future, instances of union autonomy will be sporadic and decreasing. In sum, African unions must probably face a future of increasing governmental control, supervision and restriction.

CONCLUSION

The prospect of dwindling union autonomy in Africa is probably best viewed in broad historical and comparative perspective. Historically, Western-style trade unionism came to full fruition only after the completion of the Industrial Revolution and after Western societies had undergone the profound transformation from rural agrarian community and taken on an urbanized commercial character. This radical transformation was accompanied by a whole range of interrelated socio-economic changes. Industrialization fostered the growth not only of trade unions but of a wide array of specialized associations. These groups were vital to the creation of a wholly new political culture characterized by a multiplicity of competitive interest groups, crosscutting personal ties and attitudes of restraint. Indeed, the presence of such crosscutting affiliations was probably critical to the preservation of a free trade union movement in Europe, since it was a major factor of social integration and helped foster the attitude that group differences should be worked out through a process of bargaining and compromise.

This sort of political culture has not yet emerged in Africa. Unions not only preceded full industrialization but all the other social changes which, in the West, have accompanied it. For this reason, it may be seriously questioned whether Western-style trade unionism "fits" into the culture of modern Africa. The initial argument of this chapter was that the historic presence of free trade unionism in Africa was, at least in part, the product of an artificial colonial experience, the tendency for European governments to impose on the African setting the institutional patterns of their own societies. Seen in this light, the free trade union tradition is neither a natural feature of the political culture of most African states, nor is it directly related to the special development needs of societies confronted with scarce physical and infrastructural resources. Many African leaders have already called into serious question whether the Anglo-American model of structurally differentiated institutional arrangements is best suited to the needs of African nations. Since a primary feature of the political culture of contemporary Africa is the definition of the "public interest" by political leaders, the ultimate position of the unions on that continent will depend upon how these African leaders answer the question they have posed for themselves.

CHAPTER 2   LABOR'S ROLE IN EMERGING
AFRICAN SOCIALIST STATES

William H. Friedland [†]

In a paper written some time ago,[1] this writer sought to summarize what were seen as the nascent trends in African Socialism by indicating four major developments in the social arena. These were: the development of the idea of the social obligation to work; the conversion of trade unions from "consumptionist" to "productionist" functions;[2] an orientation toward the establishment of a classless or minimally stratified society; and movement toward what was called a "focal institutional society," i.e., a society in which a single institution (the party) permeated all other institutions in society and effectively controlled their development.

While the ideology of African Socialism has retained its somewhat ambiguous quality since the time of writing, some of these nascent tendencies have emerged more clearly in terms of the behavior of the African Socialist leaders. This chapter will deal specifically with the trade unions of the African Socialist countries to examine the degree to which they have

---

[†]William H. Friedland is Associate Professor at the New York State School of Industrial and Labor Relations, Cornell University. Author of several studies on African labor, he was co-editor (with Carl G. Rosberg, Jr.) of *African Socialism* (Stanford: Stanford University Press, 1964) and author of *Unions, Labor and Industrial Relations in Africa: An Annotated Bibliography* (Ithaca: Center for International Studies, Cornell University, 1965).

[1]William H. Friedland, "Basic Social Trends," in William H. Friedland and Carl G. Rosberg (eds.), *African Socialism* (Stanford: Stanford University Press, 1964), pp. 15-34.

[2]The distinction in union functions between "consumptionist" and "productionist" is based on Isaac Deutscher, "Russia," in Walter Galenson (ed.), *Comparative Labor Movements* (New York: Prentice-Hall, 1952), p. 505.

succeeded in carrying on the productionist activities that increasingly have been assigned to them by their governments.

Two important points should be noted at the outset. First, while the discussion here will focus on the African Socialist countries, the tendencies described with respect to the trade unions can also be found--although usually less emphasized--in the non-socialist African countries. There is a difference in quality, thus, between the degree to which these tendencies occur in the socialist as compared to the non-socialist societies.

Secondly, it must be noted that there exist no hard criteria to determine which African countries can be called "socialist." The doctrine of African Socialism is fairly general and has little specific economic, social or political content that demarcates it from the actual behavior found in many African countries which make no claim to being socialist. Indeed, there is often little homogeneity between countries that are avowedly socialist. Comparison reveals that similarities and differences exist between countries irrespective of the quality of their ideologies. Thus, ultimately, the major distinction is between those countries that call themselves socialist or "African Socialist" and those that do not. For our purposes, Ghana, Guinea, Kenya, Mali, Senegal and Tanzania constitute the primary examples of African Socialist countries, and it is with this group that this chapter will be mainly concerned.

While unions throughout Africa have been captured to some extent by governments, an examination of their situation shows some differences between the African Socialist and the non-socialist countries. These deal largely with the role that the governments project for their national unions. This chapter will begin by examining the role of labor and the unions as it is conceived by the African Socialist governments. It will then turn to a consideration of the extent to which unions have been successful in fulfilling the expectations of their governments. Finally, brief consideration will be given to the role that unions project for themselves and how this relates to the expectations of governments.

GOVERNMENT'S PROJECTED ROLE FOR THE UNIONS

The political leadership of the African Socialist countries

has been acutely aware of the economic, political and social significance of the trade unions.[3] Because of their strategic location in the national economy, the unions hold an effective position relative to the modern sector. Because of their strategic location in the centers of urban population, the unions constitute a potential threat to the political leadership, particularly since they are traditionally oriented toward channelizing discontent. This position is exacerbated by growing unemployment in the urban centers. It should also be noted that the unions constituted, at the time of independence, a communications network independent of the political parties and, therefore, were capable of acting autonomously for purposes of mobilizing a crucial sector of the economy against the newly independent governments.

Thus, there has been considerable concern about the role of the unions on the part of the political leaders. Among other things, the leadership has outdone itself in creating metaphorical expressions, often anatomical in character, to describe the relations between the unions, on the one hand, and the parties and governments, on the other. Nyerere has made reference not only to the "case of the right hand helping the left,"[4] but to the unions and parties being "legs" of the same nationalist movement.[5] Nkrumah has referred to the nation as "a great tree," with the Convention People's Party acting as the roots and the trunk and the unions and other organizations constituting the branches.[6] Senghor is reputed to have referred to party and the unions as "siamese twins."

As the political leadership has come to grips with the realities of the postindependence era, it has been discovered that while unions and party may be "legs of the same body,"

---

[3]Elsewhere, I have analyzed the awareness that political leaders have of the potential of trade unions. See William H. Friedland, "Paradoxes of African Trade Unionism: Organizational Chaos and Political Potential," *Africa Report*, Vol. X, No. 6 (June, 1965), pp. 12-13.

[4]Julius Nyerere, "One Party Rule," *Spearhead*, November, 1961.

[5]Julius Nyerere, "The Task Ahead of Our African Trade Unions," *Labour* (Ghana TUC Publication), June, 1961.

[6]Kwame Nkrumah, "Speech to the 10th Annual Delegates Conference of the CPP," *Ghanaian Worker*, August 8, 1959.

they are not always marching in the same directions. Thus, the political leadership has become increasingly concerned that the unions break with the consumptionist activities that characterized them in the preindependence period and begin to make contributions to national development. Essentially this entails a considerable shift in the work of the unions, not to speak of the attitudes of the union leadership.

> The first responsibility of the unions must be to develop a disciplined, skilled and responsible labor force. African governments like ours help trade unions to become involved in economic activities such as cooperatives, housing schemes and training.[7]

The shift to productionist functions, originally motivated by the need to cut down the high strike rate, has now moved in more clearly specified directions. The projections of the political leadership are shaping up in terms of three main trade union activities: disciplining the labor force, encouraging savings and investment among workers to facilitate additional capital accumulations, and in administering such schemes as well as various social services.

DISCIPLINING FOR PRODUCTIVITY

The social obligation to work is a predominant theme of African Socialism. Not only has this been a central argument by the political leaders in speeches,[8] but it has become part of the everyday life of the country, as manifest in newspaper headlines. Thus, in Tanzania, headlines read "Work for grand design," "Be ambitious in development plans," "Slackers cheat the nation."[9] Nkrumah urges the workers "to work hard...for the economic emancipation of the country."[10] Because the unions

---

[7]Jomo Kenyata, "African Socialism and African Unity," *African Forum*, Vol. I, No. 1 (Summer, 1965), p. 37

[8]Friedland, "Basic Social Trends," *op. cit.*, pp. 16-19.

[9]*Tanganyika Standard*, February 13, 1963; February 10, 1963; June 23, 1964.

[10]Speech by Kwame Nkrumah quoted in John Tettegah, *A New Chapter for Ghana Labour* (Accra: 1958), p. 9.

organized the modern labor force in the preindependence period, the political leadership has come to see them as agents through which the government goal of greater productivity can be achieved.

Prior to independence, the consumptionist activities of the unions, concerned with raising wages and standards of living of their members, were fully consistent with the political goals of the nationalist movements. Because the colonial governments were major employers and because most employers were expatriates and identified with the colonial governments, increasing the living standards of the workers served to drain the resources of the expatriates and colonialists. After independence, the political parties took over the governments and thus became responsible for the operation of the entire economy. The political leadership now found itself in the role of employer in dealing with unions. Furthermore, responsibility for the implementation of development plans meant both increasing the productivity of labor and cutting the consuming power of workers. The unions, therefore, were now to cease their concern with extracting higher wages and better conditions from employers and begin implementing development plans by acting as disciplinary agencies. While this view of the role of unions became widespread throughout the continent, its reinforcement has been most dramatic in the African Socialist countries where, by legislation or government decree, the unions have been centralized and strengthened, on the one hand, while industrial disputes have been minimized or totally prevented, on the other. In Ghana and Tanganyika, for example, the unions were completely restructured through government legislation. In Guinea and Mali, the unions have been effectively integrated into the party structures through nonlegislative means. In Kenya, where at the time of writing no legislation has been enacted, an effective administrative takeover by government produced the dissolution of the two competing central labor organizations (the Kenya Federation of Labor and the Kenya African Workers Congress) and has established the Central Organization of Trade Unions (COTU).

While the unions have been taken over, they have been strengthened considerably, especially in financial terms. Compulsory checkoff legislation now exists in Ghana, Kenya and Tanzania. The financial strengthening of the unions does not mean, however, that they now have greater *autonomous* strength than before. Indeed, governments have taken steps to ensure that the enhanced powers of the unions do not get out of hand. In Tanzania, for example, the two main officials of the new single-union, the National Union of Tanganyika Workers (NUTA), are now appointed by the President of the Republic (Mr. Nyerere). A somewhat similar procedure is now being contemplated by the Kenyan Government for COTU.

Even where direct control through legislative means is not used, the political leadership utilizes other mechanisms to ensure the maintenance of control over the unions. In Ghana, for example, the leader of the unions, John Tettegah, was for a considerable period a member of the Cabinet. In Tanganyika, the Minister of Labor, Michael Kamaliza, was designated General Secretary of NUTA while retaining his ministership and his seat in the Cabinet. Where cooptative techniques are ineffective, governments have not hesitated to utilize coercion. Thus, an unknown number of Tanganyikan unionists remain in detention and, in Ghana, strike leaders have been jailed.

To help cut down on industrial disputes, governments have undertaken two basic strategies. On the one hand, governments have assumed greater responsibility for legislation affecting wages and conditions of employment; on the other, they have created complex procedures of dispute settlement that have effectively restricted unions from practicing traditional techniques to enforce their demands, namely strike activity. These measures have been explained in terms of the new productionist role of the unions. Thus, Kamaliza noted, for example, that wage earners constituted only about 7 per cent of the total population of Tanganyika, and the unions, therefore, must participate in national development remembering "its wider responsibilities to the community as a whole."[11]

It should be emphasized that measures restricting the consumption activities of the unions have not been restricted to the African Socialist countries. Similar developments have also occurred, for example, in Zambia and Uganda. Even in Nigeria, which has been least restrictive of the unions, the federal government has allocated official recognition to the United Labor Congress and thereby established a precedent for "un-recognizing" it sometime in the future.

---

[11] Michael Kamaliza, "Tanganyika's View of Labour's Role," *East Africa Journal* (November, 1964), p. 11.

In the African Socialist countries, however, the arguments usually get pushed further and controls over the unions have proven to be more effective than in the non-socialist countries. The positive contribution which the unions can make to development has been emphasized, as has the contention that wage earners have to transcend their own special interests to participate in a national program of development. Thus, Senghor has stated that "it would not serve the public interest to increase the disproportion between the living standards of the classes now in the process of formation,"[12] when arguing against the tendency of government workers' unions to continue to seek wage and salary increases in the postindependence period.

CAPITAL ACCUMULATION

Perhaps the most significant role being projected for the unions by the government is that of acting as an agency for capital accumulation. As consumers, workers add little to economic development of their respective countries; most African Socialist governments, therefore, have given serious consideration to using the unions to effect savings by workers-- savings which can be accumulated in sufficient quantities to permit the unions to make a contribution to capital growth. In projecting this role for the unions, the political leadership has not only been concerned to find new functions for those which have, in effect, been taken over by government (i.e., wage determination). In addition, governments have been interested in utilizing the position of the unions with respect to their constituency. Workers have developed a certain loyalty toward their unions which permits the unions to undertake responsibilities that other agencies might not be able to accomplish so effectively.

The case of Tanzania is perhaps somewhat typical. Here, even prior to the takeover of the unions and the formation of NUTA, the unions felt pressures from government to make some "positive" contribution to national development, and a Workers' Investment Corporation was sketched out. Invest-

---

[12] Leopold Senghor, *On African Socialism* (New York: Praeger, 1964), p. 56.

LABOR IN AFRICAN SOCIALIST STATES   27

ment activities were minimal, however, mainly because the financial state of the union precluded any allocation of funds for savings. Under the legislation creating NUTA, the union was charged with the formation of the Workers' Investment Corporation (WIC). Because it was intended to keep NUTA's administrative expenditures below 40 per cent of total income, the residue would be made available for investment through WIC.[13]

In addition to the intended savings to be accomplished through utilization of dues income, provision has been made in Tanzania for the establishment of a Provident Fund Scheme by which NUTA members may contribute via the checkoff. Half of the money so obtained is scheduled to be invested in government savings bonds while the other half will go to the Workers' Investment Corporation. All of these investment activities are intended to improve workers' conditions of life, not through negotiation with employers but ultimately through improving the capital base of the country and, as envisioned by NUTA's General Secretary Michael Kamaliza, through the ownership of the means of production.

> Through this means, workers in an independent Tanzania will be able to own their own factories, enjoy the products and profits of these factories and ultimately improve their own living conditions. This means, in fact, that the NUTA will, in itself, be a means toward the establishment of African Socialism. Through the Workers' Investment Corporation, NUTA will ensure that a fair share of the National Economy will be in the hands of the citizens themselves, instead of being controlled by a few individuals only as before.[14]

With these anticipated captial resources, NUTA has projected substantial investment activities in housing, shops and

---

[13] William Tordoff, "Trade Unionism in Tanzania," unpublished paper. Tordoff estimates (correctly, in this writer's view) that NUTA's annual income should exceed £300,000. This would mean, if the 40 per cent figure for administrative expenses is adhered to, that £180,000 ($504,000) would be available for investment purposes.

[14] Speech by the Hon. M. M. Kamaliza, M. P., to the first NUTA Annual Conference, March 24-31, 1965.

commercial quarters intended for rental purposes, the opening of cooperative shops in conjunction with COSATA (the parastatal consumer cooperative organization), and to build canteens for workers' use, as well as dispensaries which would make medical services available to workers.[15]

The Tanganyikan case provided a model to the Kenyan Government when COTU was recently established. Provision was made that one third of the income accruing from the compulsory checkoff system be routed to an investment fund to be approved by the government.[16]

In Ghana, while the pattern has been somewhat different, the industrial relations legislation of 1958 provided for the creation of a department through which the Ghana Trades Union Congress (GTUC) could develop its own enterprises in industry and agriculture. Out of total dues collected by the national unions, 10 per cent was to be allocated for social welfare work and another 5 per cent was to be channeled directly to a fund concerned with the development of business enterprises. In addition, the GTUC was, on its own, to charter subsidiary companies which would engage in business enterprises.[17]

It is with respect to the savings and capital accumulation function that unions in the African Socialist countries are distinctly different from those in the non-socialist countries. While concern for maintaining control over the unions has been expressed almost universally in Africa, it is the socialist countries that have sought to involve the unions in savings activities and assigned them considerable responsibilities as agencies for accumulation of capital.

ADMINISTERING SOCIAL SERVICES

When acting as agencies for the accumulation of capital or in operating provident funds and investment schemes, unions in the African Socialist countries increasingly are beginning to

---

[15] *Ibid.*
[16] *East African Standard,* September 3, 1965.
[17] Tettegah, *A New Chapter for Ghana Labour,* op. cit., p. 28.

have thrust upon them significant roles in the administration of social services. This is, in a sense, a substitute for their former function of determining wages and conditions of employment--a function which has been assumed largely by the governments. The role of administering social services is not unusual for unions in many parts of the world. Russia's unions, for example, conduct social service activities as a main part of their work. In the non-Communist world, unions in Scandinavia and the Netherlands all conduct social service activities. And even some free enterprise unions in the United States handle some social services.

While Africa's unions frequently were formally endowed with social service functions prior to independence,[18] it was only in extremely rare cases, if any, that social services were actually conducted by the unions. Most unions had enough problems surviving financially, let alone attempting to undertake social service responsibilities.

In the postindependence period, however, social service activities by the unions have increasingly been permitted and encouraged by African Socialist governments. Thus, in Mali, the labor code promulgated in August, 1962, gives unions the right to establish provident schemes, experimental farming stations, schemes for education, courses and publications, and to establish mutual aid and pension funds for union members.[19]

The Ghana Trades Union Congress (GTUC) now had undertaken a program of training cadres to give them technical skills

---

[18] In Tanganyika, for example, the model constitution prepared by the Labor Department and adopted by most unions word-for-word contained among its objects the following:
    2. Additional objects of the union shall be as follows:
       (a) To provide for members, all of any of the following benefits....
          (i) Relief in sickness, accident, unemployment.
          (ii) Old age allowances....
          (iii) Allowances in respect to loss of earnings of members arising out of a trade dispute....

[19] Mali Labor Code, Act Nos. 62067, August 19, 1962 (*Legislative Series* [Geneva: International Labor Office, 1962]), *passim*.

as well as correct political orientations. In February, 1965, GTUC initiated a series of courses aimed at creating a "new type of worker who would be in the vanguard of socialist labor and construction."[20]

Among the social services undertaken by Tanganyika's NUTA (aside from those implicit in capital formation activities) has been expansion of its education program, which will be oriented heavily toward the provision of adult education.

Aside, however, from being assigned a specific role in providing educational services, the examples cited indicate that the social service activities of the unions in African Socialist countries are still somewhat sparse. There have been discussions at various times as to the role of unions in solving unemployment problems by participating in labor exchange programs, but little has materialized in the way of specific assignments of these activities to the unions. While there appears to be a preliminary orientation in this direction, it is largely government departments that still assume the bulk of the responsibility. In Ghana, for example, it was recently announced that the Ministry of Labor would be expanded to ensure safety, health and welfare in new factories. Employment centers through which social services would be administered were to be set up in District Commissioners' offices.[21]

Thus, while, on the one hand, unions are regarded as instrumentalities for manpower development and education, and as convenient entities through which the capital they accumulate may be administered to provide social services for wage workers, on the other hand, primary responsibility for worker welfare and social services remains as yet in the domain of direct governmental actvity.

UNION RESPONSE TO GOVERNMENTAL PROGRAMS

While the three types of activities that have been discussed

---

[20]*Daily Graphic* (Accra), No. 4474 (February 16, 1965).
[21]*Ibid.*, No. 4522 (April 13, 1965).

LABOR IN AFRICAN SOCIALIST STATES   31

have been formalized in a number of places either through legislation or through the application of government pressure, the successes which have been registered in obtaining compliance by the unions have been somewhat questionable. It should be noted initially that, at least at the formal level, governments have been quite successful in creating the formal organizations which embody their policies. Thus, in Tanzania, WIC *does* exist, and in other countries similar structures have been created which provide at least the structural basis for fulfilling the roles projected by governments.

While there are serious methodological difficulties in assessing the success of governments in projecting these roles,[22] there are some indications that the programs are not viewed with wholehearted enthusiasm by the unions and their constituents. Indeed, it would appear that much of the success that has been registered to date is more a response to the coercive pressures of government than voluntary acceptance.

While only the most tentative of assessments is possible now, let us utilize the previous framework to examine the degree to which unions have adopted the roles projected for them by the African Socialist governments.

DISCIPLINING FOR PRODUCTIVITY

Whatever success there has been in reorienting the unions

---

[22]Assessment of the successes or failures of the governments' projected programs is made difficult by the degree to which news is controlled nowadays in Africa. Generally, to the extent that news appears, it focuses almost invariably upon successes. Little public information is revealed of the failures of programs or of the degree to which programs have won acceptance by union members. Thus, one must take the contention of Michael Kamaliza, speaking of house construction activities, that "our project has been accepted by *all* the workers" with some degree of skepticism (Kamaliza speech, *op. cit.*, my emphasis - WHF). The student of African development is forced to turn to a variety of sources to obtain some assessment of the degree to which the projected programs have been successes or failures.

toward productivity goals has been achieved through legislation limiting the right to strike, frequently adopted over the vigorous opposition of the unions and their leaders. Although the union leaders committed themselves to acceptance of goals of national development at an early period following independence, most were loath to surrender the main weapon which had provided them with some previous success. Even when legislation was adopted in country after country limiting the use of the strike, unionists remained obdurate and autonomous thereby leading political leaders in country after country to look to more direct takeovers of the unions as solutions to their problems. The takeover of the national centers in so many countries argues rather conclusively that the unions were either unable or unwilling to undertake the disciplining of their constituency on behalf of the government.

In Kenya, for example, strike control was initially attempted through a tripartite agreement in February, 1964, through which unions agreed to forego strikes and wage claims for one year in exchange for a specific guarantee that government and industries would increase the number of employees.[23] Nevertheless, by June, 1964, there already had been 150 strikes as compared to 230 for the whole previous year.[24] Ultimately, this situation contributed to the takeover of the two competing national trade union centers.

Similarly, even where there has been considerable government control over union activities, the existence of independent-minded unionists has been a continuing source of irritation to the governments. Unionists, for example, while often dependent upon government assistance, have not always endorsed concomitant restrictions. S. Omari, a former Kenya trade unionist, criticized the Industrial Relations Bill restricting strikes, as being protective only of employers, calling it a "product of African capitalism."[25] The response of the TFL leadership to the restrictive legislation introduced in the Tanganyikan National Assembly in June, 1962, was strongly negative.

---

[23]*Africa--Political, Cultural and Social,* February, 1964.
[24]*Ibid.,* July, 1964.
[25]*East African Standard,* April 30, 1965.

Ultimately this has led to replacement of union leaders by party loyalists. In Guinea, for example, the Executive Committee of the teachers' union was replaced following the teachers' strike in 1961. In Ghana, John Tettegah, who had established a significant measure of control over the GTUC and who was using his power as a member of the seven-man Central Executive of the CPP to push through trade union policy, was replaced by party decision in the spring of 1962. Again in 1964, the Ghanaian Government purged eight top ranking officers of the GTUC. J. K. Ampah, the new General Secretary, announced that "the recent changes taking place in the Congress were being made with one object in view, that of making our trade union movement an even more effective instrument for the consolidation of the people's power under Kwame Nkrumah."[26]

The full significance of these changes at the top echelons of the unions has not yet emerged: While they undoubtedly have some relation to attempts by the leaders to carry on traditional union activities, their explanation may also be found in internal party schisms or for other reasons. Nonetheless, there is additional evidence--albeit scattered--that the unions have failed (or are declining) to exercise discipline over their constituents. This emerges most clearly through a number of strike-demonstration situations.

In Ghana in 1960, for example, the Commercial and Allied Workers Union (CAWU) demonstrated in Accra over the delay by government in appointing an arbitrator to settle a longstanding wage dispute. The demonstration was aimed at GTUC headquarters and the National Assembly. Efforts by GTUC leaders to contain the demonstration only irritated the demonstrators, and probably it was only a promise by Nkrumah to increase wages that prevented the demonstration from expanding into a full scale strike.[27] The next year, in September, 1961, a major strike occurred in Sekondi-Takoradi because of the establishment of a system of forced savings. Here the local leadership of the unions was heavily involved in the strike in spite of strong condemnations as to its illegality by GTUC General Secretary Tettegah. In spite of promises and threats

---

[26] *African Labour News*, No. 125 (August 25, 1964).
[27] D. Rimmer, "The New Industrial Relations Act in Ghana," *Industrial and Labor Relations Review*, Vol. XIV, No. 2 (1961), p. 223.

the strike continued for 21 days. Ultimately, it ended only after an appeal and an ultimatum from Nkrumah, and 48 strikers were imprisoned as a result.[28]

While no systematic evidence is available, such examples indicate that the unions have not accepted the projected role as disciplinary agencies increasing the productivity of workers in a completely enthusiastic fashion.

CAPITAL ACCUMULATION

Where governments attempt to project forced savings activities upon workers, there appear to have been strenuous objections. The Sekondi-Takoradi strike of 1961 is a case in point. It developed largely as a protest against a scheme that would have deducted 5 per cent of wages from all workers with incomes of over £120 a year. Savings were to have been invested in development bonds earning 2.5 per cent interest but were not to be returnable for 10 years. But the strikers seemed disinterested in the national development aspects of the proposed savings scheme. The strike involved approximately 10,000 workers and required substantial intervention to bring it to an end after 21 days. Considering that the strike was heartily condemned by the national trade union leadership, the ability of the strikers to remain on strike for such a long period provides a rough index to the reactions of the workers to the forced savings proposals.

Somewhat similar sensitivity to government use of savings developed in Tanganyika in August, 1963. At that time, the government announced its intentions to take over management of the port and direction of port labor the following year. When the announcement was made, the dockworkers vociferously demanded that provident funds, then being held by the private employers of dock labor, be returned to them in cash. The considerable distrust and hostility to the intentions of the government were made clear at a mass meeting at which Minister of Labor Kamaliza attempted to address the workers. He was shouted down despite a promise of a Shs. 200 ($28.00) bonus

---

[28] *West Africa*, No. 45 (1961), pp. 1003, 1031, 1042, 1058, 1367.

for those workers who would not demand their money. In addition, workers who demanded cash were threatened at the same time with dismissal.

If the unions in the African Socialist countries have had any marked successes in accumulating capital, these successes have not been translated into tangible assets. Not only has relatively little been heard of buildings, provident and savings schemes, investments, etc., but the continued if sporadic disaffection of groups of workers from the unions would tend to indicate that union members have not accepted the functions projected upon the unions with unqualified delight. The failure of NUTA, for example, to accumulate substantial sums for investment purposes would indicate that one (or more) of the following events are occurring:

1. Workers are not paying dues and NUTA therefore does not have any money for investment.
2. Workers are paying their dues but the funds are being used almost entirely for administrative costs, leaving nothing for investment purposes.
3. Workers are paying dues but administrative problems, lack of expertise, or other organizational difficulties are preventing the unions from actually showing material manifestations of the funds accumulated.

ADMINISTERING SOCIAL SERVICES

Nor is it clear that much more substantial success has been registered in the administration of social services by the unions. While some educational programs have been operated successfully, it is less clear to what extent unions have expanded into the social services to workers.

In Tanganyika, for example, in his address to the First Annual Conference of NUTA, while Michael Kamaliza projected the construction of 3,000 houses with a required capital of Shs. 40,000,000 ($5,600,000), he reported only the construction of six demonstration houses. On its part, WIC was reported to be operating a dairy farm some twelve miles from Dar es Salaam. As the concrete embodiment of one year of activities, the successes reported can hardly be considered impressive.[29]

Nor is the success with the administration of educational schemes necessarily more impressive, since many such schemes have been operated in conjunction with external agencies such as the International Labor Organization (ILO) and/or the International Confederation of Free Trade Unions.

As yet unconfirmed reports have been heard of a demonstration occurring in Sekondi in Ghana during the summer of 1965, when a union was to have begun administering some social services involving contributions from its members. While no information has been made public, it is believed that the union's officers refused to accept these responsibilities and were involved in a demonstration which was put down by a show of force.

It is, of course, too early to attempt to assess the degree of success of failure in the administration of social services. The administrative structures necessary to handle such services are necessarily complex and difficult to get under way, particularly if there exists little experience with them. Moreover, it is evident that government policy as to the extent to which the administration of social services is to be a union role remains ambiguous. Assessment, therefore, must be considered as extremely tentative at this time.

THE UNIONS' SELF-IMAGE

That the unions have, in many cases, failed to fulfill the roles projected for them by government is hardly surprising. It should not come as a shock that unions would continue to project for themselves many of the roles which they assumed during the period of their growth prior to independence. Expectations in the colonial period, whether realistic or not, were based upon typically Western models of trade unionism which the colonial governments transmitted to the Africans (frequently

---

[29] What may be more impressive is that NUTA's first conference has been estimated to have cost the Union £200,000 ($560,000).

unwillingly). These models were frankly consumptionist and stressed that the prime function of unions was to increase the standards of living of their members. Political involvement, although it took place, was heavily denigrated, especially in the anglophonic colonies.

Reinforced by considerable successes, supported by the nationalist movements, the unions were able to win wage increases and improvements of working conditions. Union leaders not only developed experience thereby but came to value the autonomy of their social base, the urban, organized proletariat. Although unable to challenge the political leadership on political grounds, they were continually able to mobilize their followers on economic issues. As legislation undermined the utilization of traditional weapons and activities, unionists experienced difficulties in adjusting to the new demands being projected by government.

Furthermore, the rank and file has not necessarily surrendered its orientation toward pursuing self-interest goals typical of Western trade unionism. Although the upper echelons of the unions have now been captured in all of the African Socialist states, sporadic reactions continue to take place. As economic crises continue, as workers are forced to save more to pay for the visible extravagances of the political leadership, it can be expected that reactions will continue to occur from time to time.

These reactions will, in effect, be supported by the continued existence of the unions and the fact that the unions continue to play their traditional role in grievance-handling, an activity that tended to be only weakly developed in the early days of unionism but which is *probably* of increased significance today. Because the unions can no longer operate to resolve wage problems, much energy is now going into the resolution of small-scale, noneconomic disputes which are frequent in all high-density industrial enterprises. In Tanganyika, for example, the unions have now legally become involved in adjudicating dismissals of workers. In Ghana in 1960, although the top leadership could not exercise any initiative on the wage front, I was able to personally see the leadership of a national union involved in handling shop-level grievances. The protest functions of unions continue, therefore, even if they have been directed away from direct economic activities.

Thus, while the union leadership at the top level may publicly (and privately) express national goals of economic development, it is likely that a split will develop somewhere in the union hierarchy between the upper and lower echelons as the intrinsic conflict between the goals of national development and the desire of a small but crucial sector of the population to increase its standard of living continues.

Coercive measures are increasingly being used to further the goals of national development. These measures seek to restrict any union activity which might be disruptive to the economy, to centralize and control the federations and to orient their activities toward government ends. However, as the federations are centralized and brought increasingly under party control, the gap between the central power structure and the rank-and-file constituency only widens. If the rank and file come to feel that unions no longer represent them, it might only serve to increase their reluctance to assume a major share of the cost of economic development. Thus by giving to labor a political role in economic development, the African Socialist leaders may be projecting a self-defeating program.

PART II

THE ECONOMIC ROLE OF
LABOR IN NATION-BUILDING

CHAPTER **3** LABOR DEVELOPMENT AND ECONOMIC MODERNIZATION

Everett M. Kassalow [†]

Looking back on the whole of Western industrial and labor development, I think most reflective social scientists would agree that while differences were enormous between Europe and the United States, and between different European countries, certain key similarities do suggest themselves. Today, with communication infinitely more rapid, with awareness of the development process and its deliberate planning heightened everywhere, it would be absurd to believe that some generalizing was not possible.

There are limits to the generalizations one can make about the development process and, moreover, those that are made will apply with varying weight in different areas. But keeping this in mind, and injecting more than usual caution that any generalization rarely applies in *pure* form to more than any one country, we shall devote the major portion of this chapter to a comparison and contrast of labor development in the emerg-

---

[†]Director of Research, Industrial Union Department, AFL-CIO, from 1954 to 1964, Everett M. Kassalow is presently Professor of Economics at the University of Wisconsin. The author of many articles in scholarly journals on domestic and international labor, Professor Kassalow is also the editor of *National Labor Movements in the Postwar World* (Evanston: Northwestern University Press, 1963). Since other chapters in this volume deal with the political aspects of trade union development in emerging nations, Professor Kassalow has not handled the problem in this chapter. For his own treatment of the political issues, one should refer to chapter ten, "Unions in the New and Developing Countries," in *National Labor Movements in the Postwar World, op. cit.*--Editor.

ing countries.

The broad subject of labor and union development as they relate to the modernizing process in the new nations compels me to generalize in any event! The method used here is comparative, between developing areas, particularly between Africa (mainly sub-Saharan Africa) and South Asia.

Latin America will be largely, though not entirely, excluded since it apparently is at a different stage of development. Moreover, space and time limits also dictate its exclusion. For some of the same reasons the material on Asia will be largely drawn from India; moreover, the size of India and its relatively advanced industrial sectors as opposed to its over-all "backwardness" makes that country's experience significant for any general discussion about development problems in the world today. Needless to say, only some of the phases of this broad subject can be covered in any one chapter.

It seems most useful to me to concentrate on those labor developments which relate to broad, national aspects of new country development. The problem of labor force recruitment and commitment is, for example, more immediately important in this respect than the question of minimum wages and living standards.

LABOR FORCE RECRUITMENT AND COMMITMENT: THE SETTING FOR LABOR DEVELOPMENT

For the development of a modern economy as well as for the ultimate creation of any labor movement, the process of labor recruitment and commitment has an obvious and critical importance. Much has already been written about these related problems. Nevertheless, it seems most useful to examine these problems or developments comparatively; that is, to draw distinctions or important correlations between the African experiences and others.

The process of labor force commitment has obviously involved substantial difficulties in almost all developing areas.

That there has been an excessive tendency, however, to gloss over and lump together these difficulties is apparent. One notes broad African, particularly sub-Saharan, patterns as well as certain Asian patterns, particularly in the Indian subcontinent. The differences between these areas, however, have not been sufficiently highlighted.

MIGRATORY LABOR
HINDERS AFRICAN LABOR DEVELOPMENT

There seems little doubt that the process of developing a modern, committed labor force has been much slower in Africa than in Asia generally, and in India in particular.

The most singular obstacle in the road of labor commitment in Africa has been the widespread practice of labor migration. These constant movements of African labor predate the European "invasion" of Africa in some respects; but what is of interest is that these migratory movements have continued and even intensified in the face of European-sponsored industrialization. The International Labor Office has commented on this:

> ...from the beginning of the development of plantations and mining operations under European management in Africa, employers have had to resort to a labor force made up of Africans whom they have employed in a temporary capacity, providing them with lodging and food at their places of work and paying them wages considered as just sufficient for single men. Thus those workers were not able, except in rare instances, to bring their families with them; they always returned to their places of origin at the end of each period of work.

> This system which still prevails, naturally results in vast labor movements, since workers are compelled to move around frequently and sometimes over immense distances. More recently, and especially since the Second World War, increased urbanization, and the continual enlargement of the modern economic sectors--due partly to the growth

of manufacturing industries, building, and public works--have served only to intensify these migratory movements and bring new types of migration into being.

It should be first observed that in certain regions, the migration of workers has operated within the system of recruitment and labor contracts controlled by the authorities and has thus involved the taking of various measures of protection for the workers at the places of recruitment, during their journey and at their places of employment. Nevertheless, in the majority of cases, and taking Africa as a whole, these migratory movements are outside any form of control and, in fact, are the result of individuals moving on their own initiative, without previous engagement and for a variety of motives....[1]

The net result of this process has, of course, been often to make the African laborer what has been termed a "target worker." He comes to urban, industrial employment for fixed periods of time, with fixed cash objectives, and as these are achieved he returns to his village. Needless to say this was never true of all African laborers, and it is declining, but it has nevertheless been a key characteristic of millions of Africans in "modern sector" employment relationships.

This process has, moreover, tended to give many African cities a sort of unreal character. Unlike typical Western industrial urban areas, many African towns have not become centers of a permanent proletariat. Walter Elkan argues:

> ...by and large it is wrong to equate the growth of towns, which has undoubtedly taken place, with the growth of an urban proletariat. African towns

---

[1] International Labor Office, *African Labor Survey* (Geneva, 1958), p. 127. Of course, there have also always been some seasonal industries in Africa, notably in West Africa, whose very structure made migratory labor more "rational" than the employment of more committed workers.

are to be compared with Army barracks accommodating successive waves of National Servicemen, and perhaps in addition some also who have "signed on" for five years, seven or even twenty-one--but sooner or later everybody leaves. So also in these towns, permanence is exceptional.[2]

While both the ILO and the Elkan studies are somewhat old, and the pattern of labor migration has declined, the problem of commitment is still critical in parts of Africa. This past spring, I asked an East African if labor migration was still as important in his country. He noted that major changes had taken place. It was now common for two (or even three) men to hold one permanent job--with one coming to the city in the year that the other was back in the village. This represents some advance toward commitment, but it is hardly what we would judge to be a modern labor setting. Indeed, this large-scale dependence upon or existence of migratory labor is the ideal type of an uncommitted labor force. Millions of workers, year in, year out, do not look upon their jobs as permanent and do not look upon themselves as permanent members of the labor force, or the modern economy.

If one turns to Asia and particularly to India, a very different picture emerges. Despite some inevitable early difficulties, the commitment of the labor force does not seem to have been a problem of similar magnitude. Some turnover, substantial absenteeism, and greatly varying productivity have been common; but once Indian workers obtain urban, industrial jobs they cling to them with an intensity much less common in Africa, particularly in sub-Saharan Africa. Indeed, Richard D. Lambert notes that Indian workers frequently tend to be overcommitted once they have made the "break" to an urban, industrial job. They carry over the traditional notion that the "patron," the employer, has assumed a permanent responsibility for the employee and, in turn, that the employee has a permanent right to his particular job.[3]

---

[2]Walter Elkan, *Migrants and Proletarians, Urban Labor in the Economic Development of Uganda* (London: Oxford University Press, 1960), pp. 3-4.
[3]See his *Workers, Factories and Social Change in India* (Princeton: Princeton University Press, 1963), pp. 91-92.

To some extent, of course, workers in any newly industrializing society will carry over traditional ideas about job rights into their new economic situations. A similar sense of overcommitment, and resulting immobility, is reported[4] in Peru by David Chaplin of the University of Wisconsin. The practice of permanent, so-called lifetime employment commitment in the large Japanese enterprises is, of course, well known.[5]

Migrations back to the village in India are for rest, religion, ritual, and the like. But these are usually just interruptions and not returns for indefinite periods, for the worker clings to the new urban job.[6]

Actually the difficulties in recruiting and "permanently" committing a labor force seem to take an acute form primarily in Africa. Latin America, to the extent one can generalize on still skimpy material, seems to reveal no greater difficulty

---

[4]David Chaplin, "Industrial Recruitment in Peru" (mimeograph,1964), *passim*.
[5]While labor economists and sociologists usually look upon these practices or attitudes of permanent commitment as carryovers from a traditional society, it is interesting to observe the major effects of American unions in the past decade to obtain, through collective bargaining, annual employment and wage guarantees, acceptance of the attrition principle rather than layoffs to meet the impact of technological unemployment, etc.
[6]In *Labor Problems in the Industrialization of India* (Cambridge: Harvard University Press, 1958), p. 45, Charles A. Myers writes that workers on leave in their villages will use every device to fight suspension by the employer if they overstay their leave." Undoubtedly, while the average Indian industrial worker is less attached than his African counterpart to a rural base, there are always exceptions. This past summer I encountered a textile worker in a Bombay union hall who was checking with the union on what his severance pay rights were, as he prepared to sever his ties with one of the companies after 27 years of service. He was returning to take up the small farm of his father who had just died in Mangalore, hundreds of miles away.

LABOR AND ECONOMIC MODERNIZATION 47

than India (and most other parts of Asia).[7]

REASONS FOR VARYING AREA PATTERNS OF COMMITMENT

Since these varying patterns of commitment have influenced, and will continue to influence, labor evolution generally and trade unions specifically, it is useful to examine the basic reasons for these differing reactions to industrialism and the challenge of wage-employment commitment. Let me first cite the differences in population factors and particularly land-man ratios.

Even with relatively high population growth rates in recent years, Africa still shows a population density no greater than North or South America, and much less than Asia.

TABLE 1

Population Density: Africa, Asia, and Latin America

Continent	Population 1961 (Millions)	Density per Square Kilometer
Africa	261	9
Asia	1721	64
Latin America (Central and South)	218	9

Source: International Labor Office, *Second African Regional Conference, Addis Ababa, 1964: Report of the Director General* (Geneva, 1964), p. 115.

---

[7]The unpublished article already referred to by David Chaplin of the University of Wisconsin concludes that, in the case of textile workers in Peru, "our evidence suggests that this earlier stage of industrial labor recruitment... is not as difficult as it is often reported to be...." Generalizations about the "easier" process of commitment in India and Peru should be qualified by adding that industrial workers in mining or plantation jobs and in nonurban areas generally seem to show fewer differences from African workers. They appear to be less easily committed to an industrial way of life.

From the nineteenth century on, population pressure on the land seems to have been a major force in facilitating the path to an urban and/or wage-earning way of life for Asian workers, and particularly workers in the Indian subcontinent. Morris D. Morris writes of India:

> First, we must recognize that the historic balance between men and resources in most areas of the subcontinent was always precarious, and equilibrium was only maintained by the systematic working of the checks of war, famine, and epidemic. Second, we must also recognize that even before British rule a significant proportion of the continent was already landless or cultivated plots which yielded submarginal incomes. These groups apparently present in all areas of the country, had to eke out their existence by working for others....[8]

Actually, so great were population pressures in major parts of Asia that one finds Indian workers streaming southward to help man the rubber and tea plantations of Ceylon and Malaya in the nineteenth and twentieth centuries. (Chinese migration overseas also reflects, in part, population pressures on the land.)

Such was not, of course, the case in Africa. Land-man ratios were relatively favorable, and when it came to recruiting a new employee/labor force, European colonial powers had to resort, for a long period of time, to more coercive methods such as taxation, forced labor, etc.[9]

Population-land pressure was only one of the main forces which made (and make) the problem of labor force recruitment and commitment easier in Asia than in Africa. The very

---

[8]*The Emergence of an Industrial Labor Force, a Study of the Bombay Cotton Mills, 1854-1947* (Berkeley and Los Angeles: University of California Press, 1965), pp. 39-40.

[9]The literature on the "coercive" aspects of African labor development is extensive. One recent, excellent summary treatment of the subject is Elliot Berg's "The Development of a Labor Force in Sub-Saharan Africa," in *Economic Development and Cultural Change* (July, 1965), pp. 394-412.

nature of land tenure systems in most of Africa made it easier and more "natural" for the worker to maintain his claim to farm land, and a full place back in the tribe, while he was off working in the city, the mine or the plantation. Even today African land tenure systems are highly traditional in character, and it is often next to impossible for an African worker to "lose" his rights to the land. The ILO observes:

> ... the fundamental difference between the modern approach to land questions and the traditional African approach is that while the former recognizes individual rights of ownership, use and transfer, the latter sees the land as being at the disposal of the whole community. It is the source from which the whole community derives its means of livelihood and subsistence....[10]

Workers who migrate to the cities or the mines do not ordinarily sacrifice their rights to land in the African community. On returning, they once more can assert their rights. Indeed, the alienation of land is so generally hemmed in, that a man cannot ordinarily lose these rights. In part this is true because the African community, tribe, clan or family claims rights of occupancy to an area of land which is often very extensive, exceeding "any amount of land which the community or the individual, as the case may be, has ever farmed or could possibly farm...." This pattern of land ownership persists even today, although it has broken down under commercial impact in some areas.[11]

Unlike the African worker who generally has had, and still has, something clear-cut and presumably desirable to return to in the country, most Indian workers who migrated to urban or industrial employment lacked a similar "stake." By the nineteenth century, in most regions of India, land was held on an individual basis.[12] With population pressures

---

[10] *African Labor Survey, op. cit.,* pp. 51-53
[11] *Idem.*
[12] See Surrendra J. Patel in chapter IV, "Historical Background," *Agricultural Laborers in Modern India and Pakistan* (Bombay: Current Book House, 1952). There were regional variations and in some areas joint village tenure was common, but joint-ownership was not the prevailing pattern. Individual, as (continued)

building up, the phenomenon of landless, or nearly landless, workers made the transition to, and acceptance of, urban life and labor commitment much different from the African migratory pattern.

Certain low caste groups in India and elsewhere in Asia were also often landless, and many of these were eager to enter the new urban industries as these developed.[13]

Needless to say, in other respects the caste system can, and does, act as an obstacle to modern labor and industrial advance. Thus in India, and in some other countries in South Asia, many types of necessary manual work are identified with particular low castes. Indeed, "doing manual labor is the symbol of lowly status, just as not doing it is the symbol of high status...." There is also a tendency for a "specialized task in a factory to become the monopoly of a caste or regional group... It is fairly well known that in appointment to jobs in factories considerations of kinship, caste and region are relevant. Appointments on 'rational' considerations are still not many."[14]

As far as labor commitment is concerned, however, the migratory pattern of much of African labor development is largely unique. Its effects have been, and still are to an important extent, profound. It leads to "impermanence and instability in employment, low output and low wages...."[15]

---

[12](continued) opposed to community or large group, land holdings had come to prevail in a number of Asian countries by the nineteenth century. In passing, one can add that *latifundia-hacienda*, large landlord-holding systems common in Latin America, made the industrial commitment of land-poor peasants less of a problem in most of that continent.

[13]Morris, *op. cit.*, p. 86.

[14]M. N. Srinivas, *Caste in Modern India and Other Essays* (Bombay: Asia Publishing House, 1962), pp. 94-95. Srinivas may perhaps, by indirection, be exaggerating the rationality of labor markets generally.

[15]*African Labor Survey*, *op. cit.*, p. 137.

LABOR AND ECONOMIC MODERNIZATION

The direct effects of migratory labor life on unionism and the prospects for union building can be quite destructive. A group of African unionists making a study of the subject observed the following regarding migratory workers:

> ...the worker who expects to stay in any given place only a short time has no incentive to strive for higher wages and better working conditions.... The result of being on the move is frustrating, sweated labor and insecurity.... The migrant laborer has no interest in joining trade unions. The workers consider regular payment of unions dues a waste of money, because they expect to be going back to the reserves or to move into another district. They are also scared of taking part in strikes for fear of losing their precarious jobs....[16]

THE ATTRACTION OF CITY LIFE: THE OTHER SIDE OF MIGRATION

Economic development is still seriously retarded in many of the developing areas by the less-than-full commitment of millions of workers, manifested by continued adherence to patterns of migration (Africa), frequent return to native villages for family or religious observances (Asia), and the like.[17]

Yet at the same time, millions of citizens in other new nations are being drawn to the same cities without any real prospect of a decent or useful job. Everyone who visits a developing area these days is appalled by the rapidity of the urbanization process--the terrible overcrowding, slums, lack of schools and health facilities.

---

[16] International Confederation of Free Trade Unions, *Free Labor World* (Brussels, April, 1960), pp. 151-52

[17] We have not here discussed the ingrained employer attitudes on the cheapness of labor, and the willingness to put up with labor turnover as long as it means low wages--all inevitably leading to perpetuation of less-than-full commitment of millions of workers.

This is the other side of the "labor problem" deriving from the urbanization-industrialization process. In spite of its lack of appeal for some, even those with permanent job opportunities, the cities have an enormous attraction for millions of others who, caught up in the much-quoted "revolution of rising expectations," seek to escape the thralldom of traditional rural life.

Brian Crozier writes of the urbanizing phenomenon in Latin America:

> Visiting Western writers usually get moist under the collar when writing about Latin America's shantytowns, but a little perspective does no harm. It is, of course, objectively shocking to Western consciences with memories of the depressed thirties, to learn that hundreds of thousands of Cariocas live without water or sanitation. But what came before and what might come after are important too. The *favela* and the *callampas* of Santiago and the *villa miseria* of Buenos Aires offend the eye and, more persistently, the nose.
>
> On the other hand, they are symbols of progress of a kind. The ex-peasants who inhabit them lived in equally degraded conditions before moving to the big city, but without the big city's side-attractions. That, indeed, is why they moved to the big city-- for its light and its shops and, here in Rio, its beaches. As an old hand of the *favelas* told a wide-eyed newcomer on a bus, within earshot of a middle-class Carioco: "You won't believe this, but here in Rio, they bring fresh milk and warm bread to people's doorsteps."
>
> The distressing popular image of the shantytowns as places of suffocating misery is truer of some than of others and in all cases only an aspect of the truth. Buenos Aires' is worse than Rio's because its inhabitants, huddled together on flat ground have neither light nor air and babies die like flies. On the other hand, perhaps 70 or 80 per cent of the houses have television and some enterprising individuals own cars.

It is wrong to think of them as unemployed and outside the monetary economy, as one writer put it. Their labor may be casual but it brings in something, and there is no rent to pay. Some prosperous inhabitants, used to the ambiance of huddled bodies, refuse offers of decent housing, at prices they could afford, preferring to save the money or spend it. Many of them come from lonely or even desolate spots and like the crowds, stinks and all. I have heard of farmers from Paraguay, with several acres of land, who have sold up and now live in the *villa miseria* with no thought of returning to the monotony of their former life.[18]

At this point, the developing countries seem to be getting the worst of both worlds--the excessive attraction of population to the modern urban centers without, as yet, full commitment to an industrial way of life on the part of the labor force.

On balance, one must conclude that some substantial reduction of the broad migratory labor patterns, and a fuller sense of commitment on the part of both employers and employees (which should lead to higher productivity) are generally desirable if Africa is to progress more rapidly. Artificial efforts to preserve rural attachments and rights do not seem feasible. But before one assumes that commitment in Africa, or Asia, will ever be as complete as it has become in the West, it is well to remember that climatic conditions may always make for differences in this respect. The need to retreat from the cities periodically may persist indefinitely, though on a reduced scale.

Elkan argues, indeed, that the half commitment, half migratory pattern of Uganda is desirable and durable.[19] On the other hand, the ILO draws another conclusion:[20]

While much that is of value is lost in the breakdown of African tribal culture, there would seem to be

---

[18]"Latin American Journey," *Encounter* (December, 1964), p. 32.
[19] *Migrants and Proletarians...*, *op. cit.*
[20] "International Wage Structure in Africa," *International Labor Review*, Vol. 78, No. 1 (July, 1958), pp. 48, 49.

little advantage attempting to prop up the tribal system once it has ceased to respond to the economic and social needs of the people.

The system of migratory labor is sometimes defended on the ground that it eases the transition from a subsistence to an exchange economy. But workers who are neither peasants nor full-time wage earners to a large extent get the worst of both worlds, and the system imposes costs on employers, and on the economy as a whole, that keep African wages down.

The employers bear all the adverse consequences of high labor turnover and the particularly heavy expense of recruiting when the sources of labor are so far distant. The economic loss to the community as a whole includes the adverse effect of tribal agriculture and land, loss of productivity and possibilities of acquiring skill and experience resulting from high labor turnover, the great wastage of manpower involved in the constant trekking back and forth between tribe and town, and the economic consequences of the social disruption caused by the system.

Growing specialization of the African labor force and its division into a group of peasants and a group of wage earners seem to be the necessary conditions for a sustained and substantial improvement in African earnings.

AFRICA:
THE RACIAL FACTORS IN LABOR DEVELOPMENT

Before turning directly to the trade union side of new country development, I shall refer to one additional aspect of labor development, which is somewhat peculiar to Africa. Nowhere else in the developing world is the race and culture barrier between propertied groups, on the one hand, and the working classes, on the other, so critical a factor.

European and American capital penetration has been as

extensive outside Africa as within it. But it is primarily in Africa that one finds, until now anyway, a relatively small native business class. Most big business involves European ownerships, and usually management, and a native labor force.

The color question is also very real in Africa between owner and manager, on the one hand, and between workers on the other. As a result, labor relations almost always seem to have a race relations component. The problem of communication between owners--and often managers--and workers has been especially difficult in Africa.

As an illustration of the cultural barriers to communication, as they affect labor relations, Houghton tells the following fascinating story:[21]

> A large firm established close to African tribal areas and employing only Africans as machine operators commenced by recruiting African youths of 16 or 17 years of age, on the ground that at this age they would learn more quickly than older men. It was, of course, realized that within a year or two the youths would wish to leave to undergo circumcision and initiation into manhood, but it was confidently expected that when this was over they would return and work for the factory for many years. These hopes were not fulfilled. The youths were trained, left for initiation, but did not return; the labor turnover of 130 per cent per annum was crippling to the factory. Management then discovered that it was contrary to custom for an African man to perform the same job he had done as an uncircumcized lad. The factory switched to recruiting older men and, although they took a little longer to train, it soon had a stable and efficient labor force and labor turnover dropped to about 30 per cent per annum.

The net result of these deep cultural gaps and the still tenuous labor commitment of the African workers is that there

---

[21] D. Hobart Houghton, "The Problems of Labor in African Development," Chapter XI in E. A. G. Robinson (ed.), *Economic Development for Africa South of the Sahara* (New York: St. Martin's Press, 1964), p. 332.

is still no real integration between worker and enterprise in most of Africa. Guy Hunter characterizes the situation as follows:[22]

> ...the productive system developed by Europeans is characterized by one dominant fact: that there was never a real fusion between the outlook and assumptions of the employer and those of his African employees. At the personal level, there was little dove-tailing of institutions.
>
> Economically, culturally and emotionally, Africans were not identified with organized employment of the Western type and the great majority of those who experienced it were never more than a quarter or a half involved, held by a thread so tenuous and so frequently broken that the real grip which a good industrial organization can have on its members could never get a hold.
>
> It was not economically all-important to the Africans who entered it; it was not, as it is for so many in Europe, one main center of their social life, or the place where roots were put down; its atmosphere and regimen were alien and often repugnant. It was not, as it is for many Europeans, a means of expressing personality through skill. Although this situation is changing now, it is the essential background of the past.

This lack of real fusion between the worker and the enterprise is a difficult one to describe, but it is critical in the emergence of truly modern industrial structures, both on the labor and management sides. As the African countries have gained independence, some of the sense of being "outside" has probably disappeared from the minds of workers, but there is still a long way to go even to approach fully "modern" attitudes.

---

[22] Guy Hunter, *The New Societies of Tropical Africa, a Selective Study* (New York: Praeger, 1964), p. 193.

RACE AND WAGE DIFFERENTIALS

Africa is unique in another aspect of race as it relates to the development of the labor force. Almost nowhere else can one find widespread instances wherein, during the course of development, skilled worker jobs--the usual building and maintenance crafts, railway engineers, etc.--were commonly reserved for non-Africans, especially Europeans, or Indians. (Dependence upon foreign management is more common in developing areas, of course, but even here Africa is probably more dependent than either Asia or Latin America.)

This, of course, had the effect of leaving African economies more vulnerable than those in other continents on the attainment of independence. Europeans have emigrated; in other instances, for inevitably nationalist reasons, the Africans have also been anxious to push the Europeans out of the coveted skilled jobs.

The reasons for this practice of importing skilled workers from abroad seem to go back to the migratory nature of the African worker--why train workers who are not "permanent?"[23] It also would appear that attitudes of white racial superiority led management in many establishments to accept the necessity of importing the key, skilled workers needed in the enterprise.

The net result of this process, aside from its leaving many African nations poorer than other developing countries in skilled native labor, has been to create special distortions in the wage structure.[24] Not only did the usual differentials between skilled and unskilled jobs exist in the wage structure, to these were added substantial differentials to attract and hold non-Africans to Africa.

As the African countries gained independence, and even before, it became natural enough for native workers to draw invidious comparisons with the abnormally high European wages. When they actually began to take over some of the jobs hitherto

---

[23]*International Labor Review*, op. cit., p. 38.
[24]For analysis of these factors as they operated in the Northern Rhodesian copper belt, see Robert E. Baldwin, "Wage Policy in a Dual Economy: The Case of Northern Rhodesia," *Race* (November, 1962), pp. 73-87.

reserved for Europeans, African workers often insisted on taking over the same wage rate, even though it was originally based upon large displacement as well as skilled differentials. Since there is usually a transition period during which Europeans and Africans may be employed side by side, it takes a formidable employer, or government, to maintain wide differentials, to the detriment of the African, for performing the same job. Unless the differentials are maintained, however, the distortions will remain even after the Europeans have been eliminated. For high differentials for skilled workers generate pressures for large increases from the unskilled and semiskilled.[25]

TRADE UNIONISM AND MOERNIZATION

Against the background of limited commitment, continued migratory ties to the village, low levels of skill and the like, it is not surprising that trade unionism tended to emerge fairly late in Africa and has rarely attained large numbers or much stability.

What is indeed surprising is that, considering the relatively modest number of unions and union members in the new countries, so much is written about it. Within the last year, numerous articles on unionism in new nations have come across my desk from the press of the International Confederation of Free Trade Unions (ICFTU), the International Federation of Christian Trade Unions (CISC, initials of the French title, to avoid confusion with the ICFTU), Yugoslav trade unions,[26] as well as many studies on the same subject by social scientists in learned journals.

Even more surprising in some respects, perhaps, is the role which these unions are playing or seem to be playing in the new countries. The limited union movements are almost

---

[25]*Idem., passim.*
[26]Perhaps wisely and significantly, the Communist World Federation of Trade Unions (WFTU) rarely singles out unionism in the new nations as a special form or problem.

LABOR AND ECONOMIC MODERNIZATION

magically transformed into a social force far beyond their mere numbers in their various countries.

A government is apparently overthrown in Congo (Brazzaville) by a movement spearheaded by the unions. Governments in Kenya, Tanzania, Ghana, and elsewhere feel compelled to rally the strongest machinery of the state to control and reorganize their still modest-sized union movements. In other countries, the government moves in to change the leadership of the unions (e.g., Algeria and Tunisia) to accomplish some of the same objectives. All these and other moves in Africa alone have occurred in the space of a few short years since liberation.

How does one account for these reactions? It is probably true that government oversensitivity to trade union action and mere trade union presence accounts for much of this reaction. For as long as any sort of protest encounters difficulty in legitimizing itself in a new society, trade unions are likely to face serious opposition, since they are inevitably centers of reaction and protest in the modernization process.

There are other factors beyond mere numbers, however, which help to account for the importance and role of trade unions. They represent one of the earliest modern types of association, for example, to emerge in the new countries. They are also concentrated in the modern sector of the economy. Almost by definition, therefore, they will have an impact on the economy and society which is highly visible and, because, it is concentrated, often quite substantial.

UNIONS COMMITTED TO MODERNIZATION PROCESS

Without giving much thought to it, trade unions in the developing countries are almost continually committed to modernization, unlike many other tradition-based groups in the society. They are, first of all, wholly organized in the modern sectors: mines, railroads, plantations, docks, factories and in public administration. To grow and prosper, they have a stake in seeing these very same sectors advance.

A recent study of the urbanization process in Calcutta notes that very few of the new urban organizations in that city help "to bring integration of the ethnic groups through voluntary organization...." One of the few exceptions this study notes "is in the labor unions where workmen from different cultural backgrounds do unite to promote their collective interests...."[27]

It is my own experience that although tribal, ethnic, linguistic, communal, and caste factors often continue to operate when political blocs within new country unions are formed, the union as a whole tends to take in all workers in its area of competence, and thereby performs a significant service in nation-building. Even more, as unions necessarily broaden their structures from local to national organization where economic development permits or "demands," they impart an even wider national consciousness to their members.

For governments seeking to build national consciousness and national consenses, the very structure of unionism in most countries is an asset, although often not consciously appreciated. Nearly everywhere the union tends to be one institution within which many traditional ties and loyalties are broken down or at least weakened. Ordinarily the union must take the workshop, the office, the mine, or the plantation as its universe. To be successful, it ordinarily must embrace *all* the workers in that work site.

Because unions have broken with much of the traditional past, the personal needs of their members tend also to depend upon modern institutions. Improved health conditions in the cities, better housing, a sensitivity to improved schooling for themselves and their children--all these are the "natural" needs of the union members.

These needs are not always so readily translated into

---

[27] Nirmal Kumar Rose, "Calcutta: a Premature Metropolis," *Scientific American* (September, 1965), p. 102.

union programs, or union support for development. But this really is a problem for greater mutual awareness and cooperation between union and government leaders. In the absence of this cooperation, of course, unions can conceivably pose a danger to the new governments and administrations. Tending to be urban, the unions can be more quickly mobilized than most other groups; they have some modern sense of organization; they have real needs; and they can be swept up by groups in opposition to the governments.

Given the tensions of change which development inevitably engenders, it does seem that, particularly in Africa where the modernizing groups and forces are so few, where unions exist they will in one way or another be key elements in articulating these tensions. For they will speak for or against an incumbent government's programs as they meet, or do not meet, the needs and expectations of union members and leaders.

TRADE UNIONISM AND ECONOMIC DEVELOPMENT

While the role or value of trade unionism in the general modernization process is probably reasonably well understood in many of the new and developing nations, particularly in Africa,[28] its economic role is less well defined or accepted. To begin with, the very nature of the process of economic development in the new nations makes it hard to define the role of the trade union. Almost nowhere do we find the classic capitalist pattern of property ownership against which trade union demands might seem completely "normal" and be permitted their full expression. At best, there are mixed sectors; state ownership and planning play an important part in economic development. In many countries, the focus is on development.

It is not surprising that the legitimacy of trade union

---

[28] Although one African government after another has found it useful to "reorganize" or limit the trade union movement, they rarely suggest that these movements should be entirely abolished.

action has been challenged less in countries like India and Malaysia, or the Philippines, where the private sector is important in the economy, than in most other developing nations in Africa and Asia. Moreover, in the case of India (and the Philippines), a large native capitalist class makes regular, Western-style bargaining and trade unionism even more "legitimate."

Not surprisingly, in Africa the conventional brand of union-employer bargaining with which we are most familiar in the West is apparently practiced most effectively in the large, internationally owned companies. Here, with enterprise in its "classic" capitalist form, the unions can and do make their demands and negotiate a surprisingly large number of agreements. It also appears that in most of Africa, many of these large firms today "are now extremely sensitive about the image that they convey to their employees and to the public of the countries in which they operate. They, therefore, follow a carefully considered industrial relations policy which they insist their constituent elements should follow...."[29]

Many of the large foreign-owned African companies prefer to deal with unions in a very legitimate manner. For otherwise, when serious labor disputes arise, they might have to deal instead with public authorities. In the uneasy postcolonial atmosphere, therefore, unions in many foreign-owned companies are in a position to exercise bargaining power which may run far beyond their true economic strength.

In a number of instances, in fact, national governments have restrained foreign companies from offering high wages and other benefits which they could afford and are prepared to pay. The governments fear that the foreign-owned enterprises might set off a chain reaction elsewhere, including the government sector. Personally known to the author, for example, a number of large companies in French and British Africa were

---

[29] From the paper by B. C. Roberts and L. Greyfié de Bellecombe, "Development of Collective Bargaining in Former British and French Colonies" (multilithed: presented at the Research Conference on Industrial Relations and Economic Development, at the International Institute for Labor Studies in Geneva, 1964). pp. 9-10.

"cautioned" by the government not to offer or agree to as large a wage increase as they were prepared to do. On the other hand, unions have also tempered their demands in view of unfavorable repercussions these might have on the rest of the private economy (which often lacks the economic capacity, incidentally, to follow the patterns of the large companies) or within the government.

ECONOMIC PLANNING AND UNIONISM IN DEVELOPING COUNTRIES

This brings us to the heart of the economic problem, to the basic philosophy of planning in new nations and the role of trade unionism. As already noted, the planning and the establishment of a substantial government-owned or controlled sector is the typical pattern to be found in most new countries of Asia and Africa. It is this reality, rather than the private capitalist property situation, that most African unions ultimately face. For even where property is privately owned, the control or influence of the planning authorities often impinges heavily upon price and wage policies.

Without handbooks to inform us, one nevertheless occasionally gains an insight in one writing or another into what planners in new nations think about the economic role of unions in development. The clearest insight known to the author is found in the writings of Asoka Mehta, who is today one of India's chief planners. What Mehta has written would, indeed, probably be more representative of planning and trade unionism in Africa than in India. It is worth quoting:

> ... In underdeveloped countries the chief problem is economic growth, and, therefore, the major question for unions is subordination of immediate wage gains to the development of the country... Unions must educate their members to give up extra spendthrift habits of the labor class... and encourage small savings among the classes... The economic implications of much trade union behavior are twofold: (1) to restrict consumption and (2) to bring about an increase in the desired levels of production.... Any

attempt to increase consumption of the population is likely to generate inflationary pressure....[30]

While African leaders are not often as explicit on this subject, in general they hold similar conceptions. The desperate need for capital accumulation and the already great disparities between the incomes of the workers in the modern sector and those in agriculture readily lead African leaders to call upon unionized workers for sacrifice.

WAGE POLICIES IN THE NEW COUNTRIES

Collision is apparently often inevitable between, on the one hand, even moderate union pressures for wage increases, and, on the other, the demands of ministers of finance and planning for sacrifice and capital accumulation.

Only a short time ago, a more or less typical clash occurred in Nigeria which, as it happens, is less rigidly plan-oriented than most Black African states. Delivering his national budget speech in the spring of 1963, the Finance Minister opposed "any increase in purely cash income." He also noted any such "increase in salaries and wages would only benefit that relatively small section of one vast population in paid employment...."[31]

In motion on another track of government, a special enquiry (the so-called Morgan Commission) had been instituted to review the adequacy of wage levels then prevailing in the country. A number of unions which had long deferred wage claims had great hopes in the results of the enquiry. While claiming his remarks were "without prejudice to the findings and recommendations of the Commission," the Finance Minister proceeded on the eve of the publication of the report in 1964

---

[30]Asoka Mehta, "The Mediating Role of the Trade-Union in Underdeveloped Countries," *Economic Development and Cultural Change* (October, 1957), pp. 16-23.
[31]*Budget Speech 1963 by Chief the Honourable Festus Sam Okotie-Eboh, C. M. G., M. P., Federal Minister of Finance* (Lagos: Printing Division, Ministry of Information, n.d.), pp. 17-18.

to throw his weight against any general increase by calling attention to the enormous costs to the government that any wage increases would create:[32]

> One per cent increase in wages will result in an increase in the capital cost of the Federal Government program to the tune of 412,510 pounds and 137,764 pounds by way of recurrent expenditures... A wage increase of twenty-five per cent will result in an increase in the capital cost of the Federal Government program to the tune of 10,312,750 pounds and in recurrent expenditures of 3,444,120 pounds....

The Minister noted that any "increase in wages can only be financed by Government" by curtailing social services or by reducing its savings and capital expenditures. He obviously thought both of these should not be curtailed. He also ruled out the alternative of "the creation of paper money... to finance increases in wages... because of the obvious inflationary effects.... This leaves as the only avenue available the taxation revenue, and, in my opinion, it would be self-defeating to increase taxes to finance higher wages...." All this, he again added, was "without prejudice to the findings of the Commission... but the nation must know the consequences and implications of their demand."[33]

The Morgan Commission made its report in the spring of 1964 and called for substantial pay increases. When the government rejected the report, a general strike lasting thirteen days ensued. Eventually, the issue appears to have been resolved largely on the terms proposed by the Commission.[34]

The Nigerian case is cited only because it was more dramatic than some others and more clearly documented than most others because of its scope. But in many ways it is typical of the kinds of pressure and counterpressure which are so common in the new countries. Typical also of this case were union

---

[32] *Budget Speech 1964 by Chief the Honourable Festus Sam Okotie-Eboh, C. M. G., M. P., Federal Minister of Finance* (Lagos: Printing Division, Ministry of Information, n.d.), pp. 24-25.
[33] *Idem.*
[34] *Sunday Times* (London), June 14, 1964.

complaints during testimony before the Morgan Commission about the ostentatious living of the new government elite. This is a recurring echo in major African strikes, particularly when the government is in any way involved.

Strikes in Ghana and Guinea a few years back, for example, were complicated by strikers' complaints that high government officials were living at too lavish a scale. The relatively reduced importance of capitalism keeps the traditional class struggle that one usually associates with the earlier stages of industrialization to a minimum in the new African states. But a new kind of "class" conflict based upon position in the state hierarchy asserts itself from time to time.

UNIONISM AND THE PROBLEMS OF INFLATION AND EQUITY IN DEVELOPMENT

At the heart of government's resistance to union demands are often fears of their inflationary impact, as well as the argument that union members already enjoy advantageous living standards when compared with the great mass of the rural population.

It is not easy to estimate the inflationary danger. In most of the new countries a relatively excess supply of labor (especially in the burgeoning urban areas), the limited extent of union organization, the general weakness of the unions-- all these and other factors serve to reduce the direct inflationary impact of union action.[35]

The real problem is, in fact, likely to be not so much the direct inflationary danger of union wage increases in private industry, but their possible spill-over effect in the government sector, where civil service worker demands for large wage increases can disrupt government budgets. The operation of so-called dual economy wage patterns with high wages in one sector and lower wages in other parts of the economy is not

---

[35]See Paul Fisher, "Unions in the Less Developed Countries: a Reappraisal of their Economic Role," Chapter 4 in E. M. Kassalow, *op. cit.*, pp. 102-115.

unknown, however; in many countries outside Africa, high wage structures in the progressive parts of the economy often exist side-by-side with very low wages in the smaller, backward firms. A major spillover of wage increases from the large foreign-owned firms into smaller firms and/or the government may not be inevitable in the new countries. Then, too, this problem will vary from one country to another depending upon the nature of the private sector, the size of the government sector, and other related factors.[36]

The equity-inequity argument applied to urban and non-urban workers and families is readily understandable in political terms. Within this framework, of course, one can appreciate the notion of balanced income development between rural and urban groups. On the other hand, however, one must recognize that this concept runs against the historical pattern of successful economic development.

Everett Hagen has noted that the income ratio between workers engaged in manufacturing and in agriculture was typically very favorable to the former in the early phases of countries which have, until now, made a success of economic development. More significant, perhaps, this ratio became even more favorable to the nonagricultural worker as development proceeded.

Obviously, non-Western development will not necessarily take the same course as that of the West. Moreover, the present income ratios in Africa between the wage and non-wage sectors--more plausible divisions in the African situation than manufacturing-agriculture--may be somewhat more in disequilibrium than was the case at a comparable stage in Western development. A study similar to Hagen's for the Soviet bloc countries would also be of interest for comparative purposes.

---

[36]Cf. Elliot J. Berg, "Major Issues of Wage Policy in Africa" (multilithed: presented at the Research Conference on Industrial Relations and Economic Development at Geneva, under the auspices of the International Institute for Labor Studies, 1964), p. 5. According to his estimate for a group of nine sub-Saharan states, public (as opposed to the private) wage bills ranged from 23 per cent to 61 per cent of the total wage bills of these states.

TABLE 2

Trend in Ratio of Money Income per Person
Engaged in Manufacturing to that per
Person Engaged in Agriculture

Country	Early Period Period	Early Period Ratio	Recent Period Period	Recent Period Ratio
France	1815-98	1.50	1906-49	1.89
Germany	1882-99	1.42	1905-51	2.16
Sweden	1869-1901	1.81	1909-51	2.52
United Kingdom	1895	1.08	1911-54	1.46
Italy	1862-1901	.94	1906-54	1.63
Hungary	1899-1901	1.66	1911-43	2.12
Japan	1872-1902	2.29	1903-42	2.41
Canada	1880-1900	1.23	1910-53	2.03
United States	1869-99	2.17	1904-54	1.67
Australia	1891-1901	.71	1911-39	1.04
New Zealand	1901	.65	1926-36	.53

Source: Everett F. Hagen, "An Economic Justification of Protectionism," *The Quarterly Journal of Economics* (November, 1958), p. 501.

Berg estimates that in the Belgian Congo in 1958, income per capita was 3,800 francs in the wage sector and 1,400 francs in the nonwage sector. In Senegal, the wage income per capita has been estimated at twice that of traders and artisans and three times higher than the income of peasants and fishermen.[37]

But Hagen's data as well as developments in modern Japan suggest that the creation of a modern industrial labor force involves a variety of factors, including the problem of incentives for workers, some sense of sharing in industrial progress and the like. Moreover, it is possible that the superior productivity of the wage workers in the modern African sector may be proportionally even higher than the produc-

[37]*Ibid.*, pp. 8, 9.

tivity of the manufacturing worker over the agricultural worker in the early nineteenth-century stage of development, which Hagen takes as his reference point. If this is true, the higher income ratios for the wage workers would also have important economic justification.

The favorable ratios for the manufacturing workers shown in Hagen's data (Table 2, prior page) cannot in any event be attributed to unionism. It was almost nonexistent in the manufacturing industries in Western Europe, the United States and Japan during the early stage used as a base in that table.

Again, this question of an income policy in the developing nations is not purely economic. It is likely that more "attention" must be devoted to the direct economic demands of the urban and/or industrial wage earners than to the still largely tradition-bound farm sectors in the earlier, critical stages of the revolutions which are going forward in the new non-Western societies. The potential volatility of the urban "proletariat" should not be underestimated.

Looking at the problem from an over-all viewpoint, both governments and unions in the new nations would probably be wiser and more constructive to recognize that there is an inflationary danger inherent in the wage pressures of wage earners. At the same time, governments and unions should avoid any notions of a simple, rigid wage freeze. Instead, they should try to structure some controled system of income increases.

Whether the construction or application of such an income or wage policy can be accomplished best within a framework of limited free bargaining, and/or some system of government arbitration or wage boards, may depend upon circumstances in the particular country. Certainly the tendency in Africa seems to be toward greater control and regulation of the trade unions and away from freedom of action for labor.

State control over the unions can become self-defeating. Protest and strain are inevitable in the process of industrialization. In the modern world, the unions can and should operate as a lightning rod for discontent and as a constructive channel for such protest. To the extent that unions become mere creatures of the state, they are unlikely to perform this task. Protest is unlikely to disappear under these circumstances: rather it may assert itself more violently albeit less regularly.

TRADE UNIONS AND SOCIAL OVERHEAD INVESTMENT

Unions are natural allies of the government; they have mutual interests in investments in the social overhead items of development. For urban workers have an immediate stake in improved schools, health and housing facilities in the sprawling cities.

Drawing unions and union leaders into the process of planning these facilities should help to divert or sublimate union concentration on wage increases. And before anyone questions the validity of devoting a reasonable share of the budgets in new nations to social or human resource investment, he should take a hard look at the persuasive, growing literature in this field. It makes a good case for a close correlation between economic development and "social investment."[38]

UNION PARTICIPATION IN
OTHER NATION-BUILDING ACTIVITIES

Housing, training and similar problems suggest another aspect of union activity in new nations in which the constant

---

[38] For example, see Walter Galenson and Graham Pyatt, *The Quality of Labor and Economic Development in Certain Countries* (Geneva: International Labor Office, 1964). In the United States, the extensive work of Theodore W. Schultz and his school clearly reveals the importance of investment in human resources in economic development; e.g., Theodore W. Schultz (ed.), *Investment in Human Beings,* supplement to the October, 1962, issue of the *Journal of Political Economy.* For Schultz on developing countries, see "Investment in Human Capital in Poor Coun-

economic struggle "normally" associated with unions has been curtailed to a considerable degree. As constructive alternatives, of course, housing, vocational training, credit union work and the like in behalf of newly urbanized workers are obvious and particularly apt areas in which unions could make a valid contribution to society in developing nations of this sort.

Turning these tasks over to the unions, the governments in the new nations serve their own interests. For unlike the pattern of development in the West, at least prior to World War I, both political and economic development are government tasks in the new nations, particularly in Africa. Assigning training, housing and simialr tasks to the trade unions, however, governments in the new nations can avoid at least some of the inherent problems of bureaucracy and centralism.

An appreciation of this "potential" area of activity for trade unions is apparently increasing in Africa. In a recent statement on African Socialism, for example, the Kenyan Government noted the following regarding trade unions:[39]

> Government will assist trade unions to become involved in economic activities such as cooperatives, housing schemes, training schemes, workers' discipline and productivity, and, in general, to accept their responsibility.

It is difficult to see clearly the full ramifications of trade union development in the new nations of Africa and elsewhere in the years ahead. Experience to date in other parts of the world offers some guidance, but no blueprint. The special circumstances of concentrated state planning and relatively great economic backwardness, on the one hand, and rising expectations, on the other, will impose severe strain on the new nations and many institutions within them, such as trade unions.

---

tries," Chapter 1 in P. D. Zook (ed.), *Foreign Trade and Human Capital* (Dallas: Methodist University Press, 1962).

[39] Republic of Kenya, *African Socialism and its Application to Planning in Kenya* (London: African Center, 1965), p. 56.

Continued discussion can be of considerable value in defining the areas of tension and difficulty and, perhaps, solutions. But open minds can profit from the exchange of ideas and criticisms as the intricate development process moves forward.

CHAPTER 4 URBANIZATION AND
THE LABOR FORCE

Alvin H. Scaff[†]

Recently, a graduate student who had newly arrived from Ethiopia sat in the office and commented upon the changes that were taking place in Addis Ababa. Finally he said, "If economic development means giving up our traditional way of life, perhaps this is too high a price to pay for progress." Many African leaders from the younger generation, as well as the older ones trained during the colonial period, are asking if the industrial-urban ways of life that have been developed by the white man are the inevitable accompaniment of economic development.

The tutelage of the West (and perhaps also in its own way that of the East) has demanded sharp changes in the social structure if the African is to enjoy the fruits of a modern economy. The African has been told that he must learn to farm with machinery, that he must learn to live in towns, that he must take steady employment, earn more money, live with only one wife, have fewer children, work harder, and spend more. He has also

---

[†]Alvin H. Scaff is Associate Dean of the Graduate College, and Professor of Sociology and Anthropology, at the University of Iowa. He was formerly head of the Social Research Section, United Nations Economic Commission for Africa (1960-61); team leader of the Urbanization Survey Mission for the United Nations, Africa (1961); and team leader, United Nations, Urban Development Mission, Kampala, Uganda (1963-64). He is the author, with team members, of *Recommendations for Urban Development in Kampala and Mengo* (New York: The United Nations, TAO/Uganda/1, 1964), and a number of scholarly articles.

been told to forget his old gods, pay less attention to his tribal chief, obey the laws of the new national government and pay more taxes. In resistance, the African has not discarded his ambivalent feelings about economic development because he is not sure that cherished elements from his own society must be sacrificed in the cause of progress. He wants at least some of the fruits of a modern productive economy, but he wants them on his own terms.

Are these reservations on the part of Africans realistic? While granting the necessity of making some changes, is it possible to accommodate old and new elements in a viable economy? Is traditional society to be understood purely as a roadblock to progress?

After nearly a generation of postwar experience in attempts to modernize traditional economies, we are now beginning to admit that it is not only impossible but actually undesirable to try to sweep away the traditional culture as preparation for economic development. Modern economy does not rise out of the ash heap of tribal society. We should recognize that out of the traditional societies come the basic structures of order, meaning, security and motivation that are needed for the great effort to create a new economy. As the new order is created, the old may be covered over or modified, but, as Durkheim observed, "without ever completely disappearing."[1]

The test of the force of these traditional structures is to be found in the towns and cities, where the greatest erosion of traditional society could be expected. Actually, we find even here that cities are not entirely in opposition to traditional society, but rather are places of cultural syncretism, societal adjustments and ethnic assimilation. In any critical examination, therefore, of social change in Africa--and we should claim that economic development is simply a special case of the larger process--we must observe carefully the social structure of cities and the part played by traditional society in the process of urbaniza-

---

[1]Emile Durkheim, *The Division of Labor in Society* (Glencoe Ill.: The Free Press, 1933), p. 229. For a sympathetic treatment of the traditional society as a force for economic development, see Gideon Sjoberg, "Political Structure, Ideology, and Development" (Bloomington: Indiana University, Department of Government, 1963).

tion. We shall assess the trends of urbanization generally in Africa, and then examine in detail a selected urban area in Uganda's capital.

AFRICAN URBANIZATION IN PERSPECTIVE

While concerned with the importance of Africa's increasing urbanization, we must note that it is the least urban of the various world regions. Figures for the percentage of the total population living in urban localities of 20,000 or more inhabitants around 1950 show Africa with 9 per cent, compared with 13 per cent for Asia and 24 per cent for Latin America.[2] However, demographers at the Economic Commission for Africa point out that this is about the same level of urbanization as that attained in Europe 100 years ago.[3] Furthermore, it is necessary to observe that the rate of urbanization in Africa is increasing. In the period of 1800-50, the annual rate of urban growth in Africa was less than 1 per cent per year; for the fifty-year period since 1900, it was 4.1 per cent per year. The average for the last 150 years is 3.9 per cent per year, equal to the urban growth rate for America over the same period of time, and ahead of the urban growth rate of any other world region.[4] At this rate Africa will not long continue to be predominantly rural with only a small urban population. Universally, the urban increase is greater than that of the population as a whole; currently in most African countries it is estimated that urban growth is double the rate of total population increase.

Variations in the level of urbanization from one African country to the next are great: U.A.R. (Egypt), 29.1 per cent in towns of 20,000 or over; Republic of South Africa, 32.9 per cent; Chad, 1.0 per cent. The growth of towns in the countries of tropical Africa has come mostly since the end of World War II, but when measured by per cent living in towns of 20,000 or more the national pictures are quite varied:

---

[2]United Nations Economic Commission for Africa, "Study on Recent Demographic Levels and Trends in Africa" (File No. SOC 200), Table 24, p. 77.
[3]*Ibid.*, p. 33.
[4]*Ibid.*, Table 26, p. 81.

TABLE 3

Level of Urbanization in Selected African States

African State	Per Cent Urban	Census Year
Congo (Leopoldville)	9.1	1959
Kenya	3.8	1948
N. Rhodesia	16.8	1960
Senegal	19.0	1956
Tanganyika	3.3	1957
Uganda	0.4	1959

Source: United Nations Economic Commission for Africa, "Study on Recent Demographic Levels," *op. cit., passim.*

Examining closely the situation in Uganda, we find that the figure of 20,000 is not realistic as a dividing line between urban and rural. A more realistic dividing line for Uganda, and perhaps for other African countries, would be towns of 500 or more, as even these smaller places contain largely nonagricultural occupations in trades, services, crafts, and small industries. Based upon this figure, the urban population of Uganda in 1959 was 5 per cent of the total. While Uganda's total population was increasing between 1948 and 1959 at the rate of 2.5 per cent per year, her urban population was growing at an annual rate of 6.3 per cent. At this rate, in 20 years the urban population will be over 10 per cent of the total and in actual numbers more than 3 times the present urban population.[5]

The rapid urbanization of Africa provides one answer to some of the questions that commonly have been raised concerning labor supply and the prospects for economic development. As recently as 1956, Lord Hailey wrote, "one of the most insistent of the problems which present themselves is that of the shortage of manpower within reach of the major industrial centers and the consequent wide prevalence of the system of 'migrant' labour."[6]

---

[5] Author's estimates based upon the Uganda Censuses of 1948 and 1959.
[6] Lord Hailey, *An African Survey* (London: Oxford University Press, 1963), p. 129.

Times have changed! Gone are the days when entrepreneurs had to mount campaigns to entice Africans into towns in order to recruit them for employment in industry or government. The African is moving into urban centers of his own accord, taking employment, and remaining in towns for longer periods of time. Undoubtedly there are variations in the extent of rural-to-urban migration from one African country to another, and also variations in the nature of employment problems produced by the migrant laborer. A recent article by Aaron Segal in *Africa Report* deals with the serious problem of unemployment in Kenya, where the urban population is growing at the rate of 6 per cent per year compared with a 3 per cent rate for the total population. But Segal notes that the same problem of unemployment does not exist in Uganda and Tanzania, where the migrants are not so concentrated, nor jobs for the moment so scarce.[7]

Migratory labor does not have a fixed function in its consequences for an economy; it may produce a wasteful and costly labor supply or troublesome unemployment which burdens urban institutions and strains the economy of a country such as Kenya. On the other hand, under other conditions the migrant laborer may fill a seasonal need, or linger and become a relatively permanent urban resident and a useful worker in the economy. Walter Elkan, in his study of urban labor in the economic development of Uganda, while underlining the persistence of migrant labor, has stated that its alleged impediment to economic growth is exaggerated.[8] Elkan points out that travel in Africa has become easier, more efficient and cheaper, and therefore the costs of labor moving from one place to another are reduced. He adds that the twin considerations of training and higher income tend to keep labor attached to a job for longer periods of time and thus reduce the expense to employers of training a new labor force. Finally, he points out that the argument that migratory labor deprives agriculture of its most virile element overlooks the contribution in savings and skills that urban workers return to agriculture. As economic development is fundamentally stimulated by rising land values, this basically desirable condition is furthered by the movement of laborers from farms to city and the return of savings from urban employment in the form of investments on the land. Elkan shows that this process is under

---

[7]Aaron Segal, "The Problem of Urban Unemployment," *Africa Report*, Vol. X, No. 4 (April, 1965), p. 17.
[8]Walter Elkan, *Migrants and Proletarians* (London: Oxford University Press, 1960), p. 129.

way in Uganda.[9]

Our thinking in the West about the urban laborer is fundamentally shaped by the peculiar circumstances of English and American experience, where the newcomer to the city was usually a landless as well as penniless individual. He had no other alternative but to take urban employment and make the best of it. The African situation is different; many of the African migrants have land, either freehold or tribal, which affords them at least a minimum income and security which can be affected little or not at all by the ups and downs of the modern world economy and its wage system in the towns. The Africans do have an alternative; they can try out the wage economy and the accompanying urban life, while they keep a firm stake in the traditional economy and tribal agriculture. As we shall show, a large number of Africans are doing just this: living in town, maintaining a household and usually also a family on traditional land holdings, adding income to income; in short, living in two worlds and making the best of both.

There is no evidence that such arrangements are harmful or uneconomic; on the contrary, the African so far has largely avoided the worst ills of urban slums as we know them in the West or as they exist in Asian cities. His continued roots in tribes and traditional agriculture provide security without burdening new economies, and the possibility of a minimum existence on wages that otherwise would be absolutely insufficient to support life in the towns. J. A. K. Leslie in his *Survey of Dar es Salaam* reports that men come to the city and live with relatives, engage in odd jobs, work only a part of the month, and then are not forced to return to farm or village when they are out of employment.[10] This kind of flexibility may be peculiarly African, as it stems directly from the symbiotic relationship that exists between traditional and urban social structures.

The desire to save, which Elkan reports was a constant theme running through his interviews with African workers in Kampala,[11] is strongly intertwined with traditional African

---

[9]*Ibid.*, pp. 131-40
[10]J. A. K. Leslie, *A Survey of Dar es Salaam* (London: Oxford University Press, 1963), p. 5.
[11]Elkan, *op. cit.*, p. 43.

society. The African wants money to buy more land, or to make improvements on his farm, or to pay taxes. He needs to buy soap and salt and occasionally renew his clothes; and these wants, rooted in his traditional society, lead him to town and into employment for a wage. No matter how little he may earn, he saves part of this for the purposes that led him into the town in the first place, and thus the process of saving and investment is initiated by the joining of urban activity and opportunity to the motives that originate in traditional society.

Once a part of the urban world, the African is not "detribalized," but, as Gluckman has pointed out,[12] is oriented to the new urban environment, making use of his tribalism to meet new problems. The new elements in his personality are simply laid down on top of the old. In the towns the great variety of goods stir his wants and multiply his desires. For example, his wants expand to include a portable radio, a striped shirt and a bicycle.

This last item has played a singularly significant role in the economic development of Uganda and perhaps other African countries. It has been used sometimes for purposes of courtship, but primarily the bicycle is the means of permitting its owner to live in the country and work in the town. Cyclists by the hundred clog the main roads into Kampala before work each morning, then stream back to the countryside each evening. The city is dominated by Africans during the day and largely vacated by them after dark. The bicycle is the mechanism linking the traditional and urban worlds and extending the geographical area around the towns where this linkage is made in the course of a daily rhythm of traffic.

THE AFRICAN SOCIAL STRUCTURE AND LABOR

As we found that the supply of labor and its function in an economy are significantly (though perhaps not in measurable quantitative terms) affected by the social structure, a careful examin-

---

[12] M. Gluckman, "Anthropological Problems Arising from the African Industrial Revolution," A. W. Southall (ed.), *Social Change in Modern Africa* (London: Oxford University Press, 1961), pp. 68-70.

ation of African social structure, especially in the urban setting, is necessary. A growing number of surveys are available on African cities. There was a major compilation of studies under the auspices of UNESCO in 1956 titled, *The Social Implications of Industrialization and Urbanization in Africa South of the Sahara*.[13] Another volume of studies, *Social Change in Modern Africa*, edited by Aidan Southall in 1959, is more concerned with social structures in towns.[14] A recent book by Hilda Kuper deals with urbanization in West Africa.[15] More specialized surveys have appeared on Kampala,[16] Jinja,[17] Dar es Salaam,[18] Luanshya (copper belt),[19] Monrovia,[20] Lagos,[21] Livingstone,[22] Sekondi-Takoradi[23] and "Caneville" (South Africa).[24] As a result of the diligent work of these and other scholars, a wealth of material on African towns is now available for use by the discerning administrator faced with the problems of government,

---

[13] Daryll Forde (ed.), *The Social Implications of Industrialization and Urbanization in Africa South of the Sahara* (Paris: UNESCO, 1956).

[14] A. W. Southall, *op. cit.*

[15] Hilda Kuper, *Urbanization and Migration in West Africa* (Berkeley: University of California Press, 1965).

[16] A. W. Southall and P. C. W. Gutkind, *Townsmen in the Making* (Kampala: East African Institute of Social Research, 1957). Also P. C. W. Gutkind, *The Royal Capital of Buganda* (The Hague: Mouton and Company, 1963).

[17] Cyril and Rhone Sofer, *Jinja Transformed* (Kampala: East African Institute of Social Research, 1955).

[18] Leslie, *op. cit.*

[19] Hortense Powdermaker, *Copper Town: Changing Africa* (New York: Harper & Row, 1962); also, Arnold L. Epstein, *Politics in an Urban African Community* (Manchester: Manchester University Press, 1958).

[20] Merran Fraenkel, *Tribe and Class in Monrovia* (London: Oxford University Press, 1964).

[21] Peter Marris, *Family and Social Change in an African City* (Evanston: Northwestern University Press, 1962).

[22] Merran McCulloch, *A Social Survey of the African Population of Livingstone* (Manchester: Manchester University Press, 1956).

[23] K. A. Busia, *Report on a Social Survey of Sekondi-Takoradi* (London: Crown Agents, 1950).

[24] Pierre L. van den Berghe, *Caneville* (Middletown: Wesleyan University Press, 1964).

industry or labor. A selection from the many studies is made with respect to our own special interests.

For our purposes of observing the impact of urbanization upon economic development, it is useful to know the direction of change as well as the structure of urban life at any given moment in time. With this purpose in mind, we shall concentrate attention upon one area in the Kampala urban complex, where it has been possible through the agency of the United Nations Technical Assistance Mission to Uganda, with the assistance of the East African Institute of Social Research at Makerere College, to make a restudy of the same area covered by Southall and Gutkind in 1954 and reported in *Townsmen in the Making*. The restudy was conducted in 1964, 10 years later, in conjunction with the work of an urban development planning mission, which was interested in urban renewal for Kisenyi, a part of the African inner city along the border between the adjacent urban towns of Kampala City and Mengo Municipality. As the area covered by the two studies was the same, it is possible to make accurate comparisons on many of the items observed by both survey teams. The results undoubtedly cannot be applied in all details throughout Africa; however, the pattern of urban social structure, the persistence of traditional elements, and the direction of change may be instructive and interesting to students of urbanization elsewhere in Africa. [25]

The 80-acre area surveyed in 1954 and again in 1964 had increased its population from 2,914 to 4,847, or 66.3 per cent in 10 years. The density had risen from 36 per acre--a low for urban development--to a crowded 61 per acre, for almost all of the structures were one level only, and new building had not kept pace with population growth. In 1954, some 16 per cent of the households were crowded with more than 2 persons per room, whereas the figure in 1964 was 28 per cent. The number of single individual households declined significantly from 36 per cent in 1954 to 19 per cent in 1964, while there was a significant increase over the period in 4 to 6 person households.

---

[25]Alvin H. Scaff, *et al.*, *Recommendations for Urban Development in Kampala and Mengo* (New York: The United Nations, TAO/Uganda/1, 1964), Chapter V and Appendix B.

TABLE 4

Percentage of Households by Number of
Persons in Each Household, Kisenyi,
1964 Compared with 1954

Number of Persons in Each Household	Percentages in Each Size Household	
	1964	1954
1	18.7	36.1
2	36.8	39.2
3	15.5	15.7
4	14.5	4.9
5	8.0	2.5
6	2.5	.5
7	2.5	.5
8	.8	.4
9	.0	.0
10	.2	.1
11 or more	.5	.1
Totals	100.0	100.0

Source: Alvin H. Scaff, *Recommendations for Urban Development in Kampala and Mengo*, (New York: United Nations, TAO/Uganda 1, 1964), p. 152.

While the area in 1954 was devoid of paved streets and through traffic ways for automobiles, a modest improvement had made the area more accessible to traffic in 1964. The area still gave the appearance of a slum. Only a few structures were built of permanent materials; most were mud and wattel, while a few were constructed of wood. Newly applied building restrictions meant that the worst of the mud and wattel houses were no longer permitted, and generally the area was less unsightly than 10 years earlier. Under a one-year-old municipal government, combining the office of Gombololo (district) Chief with that of Town Clerk, Kisenyi was experiencing the wholesome effects of regular garbage collections and policing.

As characteristic of other urban populations, Kisenyi has a

small percentage of children and a relatively large adult population in the working years. The shift in age structure is significantly in the direction of a more normal population; that is, a larger proportion of children, which makes for a more stable family-based population, even though it means an increase in dependents and a reduction of those in the working years.

TABLE 5

Distribution of Kisenyi Population by Age Groups

Age	Per cent, 1954	Per cent, 1964
0-4	9	17
5-14	9	10
15-44	76	66
45-over	6	7

Source: Scaff, *op. cit.*

Of the increased number of school-aged children in Kisenyi, we found that 70 per cent of them were attending school and that this was notably higher than the figures for Uganda as a whole. Furthermore, there is a marked upward shift in the educational level of the population of Kisenyi between 1954 and 1964, from 1 per cent to 7 per cent that have now attained more than primary schooling. Relatives of the present population of Kisenyi, that is, children or close kin, who live elsewhere, either in Uganda or outside, total 1,371, of which 426, or some 31 per cent, are of primary school age. Many of these are in school where they reside (390 out of the 426); therefore, it is clear that if families were united in Kisenyi, it would mean a large increase in the Kisenyi school population. It is also clear that the larger and more traditional family structure is widely employed in the rearing of children and their care while they are in school, and that this family structure ameliorates the load that otherwise would fall more heavily than at present upon urban institutions.

TABLE 6

School Attendance in Kisenyi and All Uganda

Schooling	Kisenyi Per cent, 1964	Per cent, 1954	Uganda African Census Per cent
None	41	40	70
P1-5	34	50	25
P6-8	18	9	4
P9-over	7	1	1

Source: Scaff, *op. cit.*

Household and family arrangements in Kisenyi were reported by Southall and Gutkind in 1954 to be variable and complex; however, statistics on these arrangements were not reported so as to provide a basis for accurate comparison 10 years later. They reported that "it was often difficult to decide who were the exact occupants of a room because of constantly fluctuating marital arrangements, and also because a number of people keep two houses going at the same time."[26] The 1964 survey did not confirm this extreme instability in households; but we did find, as had the previous authors, that "a number of urban workers have secondary wives in the country, with whom they spend the weekends, and businessmen often have wives at different places which they regularly visit in the course of their work."[27] Marital status for the adult men in 1964 showed a large proportion unmarried.

TABLE 7

Marital Distribution of Kisenyi Adult Males in 1964

Marital Status	Per cent
no wife	30.0
one wife	54.5
two or more wives	15.5

[26] Southall and Gutkind, *op. cit.*, p. 41.
[27] *Idem.*

Very few of the men with 2 or more wives had them living together in Kisenyi; in 92 per cent of such cases the second wife, or wives, lived outside Kisenyi and often outside Uganda. About half of those with more than one wife were engaged in occupations that required traveling. There is no significant relation between plural wives and the Muslim religion, which legalized such arrangements.

TABLE 8

Kisenyi Plural Marriages by Religious Faith

Religion	Per cent
Protestant	27.0
Catholic	11.7
Muslim	6.5

Source: Scaff, *op. cit.*

Significantly, among the monogamous families in Kisenyi, 53 per cent had a second house located outside of Kisenyi. This almost always implied a small rural holding and supplemental income, or potential income, should the town dweller lose his stake in the urban world. Connections through tribe and kinship between the urban and traditional world are numerous. Some 46 per cent of the households in Kisenyi include individuals not members of the nuclear family, and of these "outsiders" 7 out of every 10 are kinsmen, while the others are usually from the same tribe.

Of all the residents in Kisenyi, 54 per cent own property (land or buildings, or both). Only 5 per cent own property in Kisenyi, while 49 per cent own property elsewhere. These ownership arrangements follow closely the place of origin of the owners, most of whom come from outside of the local district.

TABLE 9

Distribution of Kisenyi Property Owners by Origin

Origin of Owners	Per cent
From outside of Uganda	48
From Uganda, outside Buganda	16
From Buganda	36

Source: Scaff, *op. cit.*

Although the non-Ugandans are numerous in Kisenyi and many still have property elsewhere, few plan to go back to their native country. When asked about plans for future residence, 86 per cent of all the residents indicated that they had no plans to move away from Kisenyi; 7 per cent said they would change if they got a better job; 4 per cent would move to secure a better house or environment; 1 per cent for the sake of children or family; and only 2 per cent said they would return to their home country. The reasons for moving to Kisenyi in the first place were largely job and occupation, which applies to 59 per cent of the cases. Another 27 per cent said they moved to Kisenyi because they found housing there at rents they could afford; while 14 per cent came because of family ties. There is no comparable information from the 1954 survey, but it appears that the African population in Kisenyi thinks of its future largely in terms of urban residence with whatever supplements and added security can be obtained from rural holdings.

The tribal complexity of Kisenyi was still great in 1964 when representatives from 30 different tribes were interviewed. This compares with some 40 tribes represented in the comparable survey in 1954. A coalescing of language skills seems to have taken place during the 10-year interval, for in 1964 almost all the interviews could be conducted in Luganda or Swahili, while 10 years earlier, the survey required the use of another half-dozen tongues.

The development of common language skills is probably related to the longer length of residence of Kisenyi's present population. Mobility is still high, but the percentage of those who have lived in Kisenyi more than 3 years has increased, and there is evidence of a stable core of long-term residents. The comparison for the two periods follows:

TABLE 10

Distribution of Kisenyi Inhabitants by Length of Residence

Years of Residence	Per cent, 1954	Per cent, 1964
Under 1	28.4	28.0
1-2	30.2	22.1
3-4	12.9	15.1
5-6	6.6	8.7
7-8	4.5	7.3
9-10	2.9	3.9
11-20	9.1	10.8
21-over	5.4	4.1

Source: Scaff, *op. cit.*

Although some of Kisenyi's employed residents work elsewhere in the larger city of Kampala, a good 42 per cent are employed within Kisenyi itself, where there is an open market for fresh produce and another for charcoal, the most popular fuel. Along two of the streets are small shops which carry a variety of inexpensive merchandise. Also located in the area are small, marginal, industrial operations, such as woodworking, shoe repair, metalworking, and auto repair. Living accommodations are located above or behind these stores and shops.

In 1954, Southall and Gutkind listed 17 occupations for the self-employed in Kisenyi; in 1964 we found 60 different occupations, and eliminating those not "self-employed," it appears that in the 10 years, the occupations have doubled in number. There is a wide distribution of the adult population among the 60 occupations; other than homemaking, which accounted for 28 per cent of the total, there were only 6 other occupations whose percentage of the total ran above 3. Notable changes had occurred in the occupational structure during the 10 years. In 1954, beer sellers were the largest single occupational group in Kisenyi (15.1 per cent);[28] by 1964, they constituted only 6.3 per cent of the total--omitting homemaking, students, and unemployed from the percentages for purposes of comparability. There was no automobile driving listed as an occupation in 1954, but by 1964, it constituted 7.2 per cent of the employed adults. By 1964, Kisenyi had become the place of residence for a small number of Africans in the professions, such as teacher, lawyer, journalist.

The occupational changes indicate the increasing urbanization of the African population, its rapid absorption into the larger economy of the city and its utilization of that economy within its own immediate neighborhood. In 10 years, Kisenyi had become more complex, more developed, and its population more highly skilled. However, traditional organization still played a significant part in occupational alignments. Members of the same tribe tend to stick together in the same occupations, and those in the same kind of employment tend to live together or in houses nearby.

Comparisons of income are difficult because the figures from the two surveys are of questionable accuracy. Information from the interviews and records compiled by the survey team in 1954 indicate a median income somewhere between 50-100 shillings per month. Some 42 per cent reported incomes at the 50-shilling amount or less, while at the other end of the scale, 3 per cent reported incomes over 400 shillings a month. Although this report of income was considerably higher than that indicated by government surveys for Uganda as a whole, the survey team working in Kisenyi said of its own findings, "There can be no doubt that they are an underestimate."[29] In an atmosphere threatened by increasing taxation, our interviewers in 1964 were able to get no information concerning income reliable enough to report. We therefore resorted to an analysis of graduated income tax returns for persons living in Kisenyi. These figures indicate a median income between 100-150 shillings per month, with 25 per cent receiving less than 100 shillings and 9 per cent in the bracket above 400 shillings per month. Although it is impossible to determine the accuracy of these reports, it is

---

[28]*Ibid.*, Table XI, p. 239.
[29]*Ibid.*, p. 52.

safe to conclude that they are conservative and that income in Kisenyi has increased over the 10-year period in line with the known increase in wages generally in Uganda, and that this increase has been in the amount of about 50 shillings per month in the lower income brackets, more for those in the higher brackets.

Rent, more reliably determined, has likewise gone up. A comparison indicates that rent has about doubled during the 10-year period. The rise in levels of rent gives credence to the comparison made between incomes and the estimates in the amount of increase in incomes over the recent decade. Together with the picture of the expansion of Africans into the more skilled occupations, these statistics on rising incomes and increasing rent levels show a population increasingly participating in the urban economy and in the rising level of living which it affords.

TABLE 11

Rentals in Kisenyi in 1954 and 1964

Rental	Shillings per month	
	1954	1964
Median rent	15	25
Average	15	25
Average for one room	10	24
Average for two rooms	21	40

Source: Scaff, *op. cit.*

The accommodation to urban life and the increasing participation in the modern economy which we observe taking place in Kisenyi occur in a context of competing groups and conflicting interests. We have noted that some 30 tribes are represented in Kisenyi, yet the dominant influence is that of the Muganda, who account for 40 per cent of the total. Also, it is important to remember that Kisenyi and the total urban complex of which

TABLE 12

Occupations, All Adults 16 and Over, Kisenyi, 1964

Occupation	Per cent	Occupation	Per cent
1. Homemaking	22.4	32. Layreader	.2
2. Student	1.7	33. Mason	.9
3. Unemployed	2.3	34. Mechanic	6.4
4. Auto driver	4.5	35. Milk peddler	.1
5. Barber	.9	36. Musician	.9
6. Barmaid	1.5	37. Newspaper seller	.2
7. Bar owner	.3	38. Office boy	1.0
8. Bartender	.6	39. Painter	1.1
9. Beer seller	3.6	40. Peasant farmer	.4
10. Building contractor	.6	41. Petrol station attendant	.1
11. Butcher	1.3	42. Policeman	1.5
12. Carpenter	1.8	43. Prison guard, etc.	1.7
13. Charcoal seller	2.8	44. Restaurant cook	2.5
14. Chicken seller	1.8	45. Restaurant owner	.4
15. Clerk-typist	3.2	46. Salesgirl	.1
16. Cooked food seller	1.0	47. Scrap dealer	.2
17. Electrician	.4	48. Shamba boy	.5
18. Factory worker	1.4	49. Shoe repair	.9
19. Fish seller	1.5	50. Shopkeeper	2.4
20. Hawker	3.9	51. Shop assistant	1.9
21. Headman or foreman	.9	52. Stall seller	1.1
22. Home industry, mats, etc.	.2	53. Tailor	2.5
23. Hotel keeper	.1	54. Teaching	.9
24. Hotel & restaurant worker	.3	55. Tonboy (loader)	.4
25. Houseboy	4.3	56. Trader	1.0
26. Housegirl	.4	57. Transporter	.4
27. Journalist	.4	58. Veterinary assistant	.1
28. Landlady	.6	59. Water peddler	1.3
29. Landlord	.2	60. Watchman	1.3
30. Laundry	2.5	61. Watch repair	.1
31. Lawyer	.1		

Source: Alvin H. Scaff, *Recommendations for Urban Development in Kampala and Mengo* (New York: United Nations TAO/Uganda 1, 1964), p. 153.

URBANIZATION AND THE LABOR FORCE   91

it is a part lie within the boundaries of Buganda, which exerts its strong traditional influence on the area. The nature of this traditional structure in Buganda is therefore quite important in shaping the changes toward modernization. Muganda traditions have proved to be notably receptive and adaptive, as observed by David A. Apter in his study of political power in Uganda.[30] Such flexibility may be traced to the complexity of Muganda social structure as shown in L. A. Fallers' *The Kings Men*,[31] or to the unresolved conflicts between interest groups among the Muganda as shown in Gutkind's study of local government, *The Royal Capital of Buganda*.[32]

    Bypassing the inviting debate over Apter's thesis that the Muganda absorb change so as to strengthen and not weaken their traditional system, we may conclude as to a minimum observation that such a traditional system is permissive of change. For example, under the impact of urban conditions and the economic opportunities created for more intensive use of land in the urban economy, the traditional tenancy arrangements and the regulation of such arrangements under the Busulu and Envujo Law have been replaced. Parcels have been divided and subdivided as tenants have been multiplied and the income from rents increased. While the process, as illustrated in the two accompanying tables, has been going on around Kampala for at least two decades, in Kisenyi the transformation of land tenure has been complete.

    The income from room and house rent motivated plot holders to construct additional buildings for which the landlords then learned to charge a "premium." Extralegal contracts and agreements have been many and ingenious, as the African has attempted to fill the widening gap between the traditional order, where investment was essentially limited to land, and the new economy, where income derives from many forms of capital investment, land being only one of them. The result has been a more complex social structure where, according to Gutkind, "new economic opportunities have strengthened the Ganda traditional elite economically, but not always politically as well."[33]

---

[30]*The Political Kingdom in Uganda* (Princeton: Princeton University Press, 1961), pp. 104-105.
[31](London: Oxford University Press, 1964).
[32]P. C. W. Gutkind, *op. cit.*, *passim*
[33]*Ibid.*, p. 272.

TABLE 13

Number of Customary Holdings in Four Kibuya Parishes,
by Distance from Kampala's Western Boundary: 1938 and 1956

Parish and Distance from Boundary	No. of Customary Holdings 1938	1956
Parish A 1 Mile from Kampala Boundary	170	59
Parish B 2 Miles from Kampala Boundary	220	95
Parish C 3 Miles from Kampala Boundary	260	125
Parish D 3-1/2 Miles from Kampala Boundary	210	141

Source: P. C. W. Gutkind, *The Royal Capital of Buganda* (The Hague: Mouton and Company, 1963), p. 180.

TABLE 14

Average Size of Customary Holding in Four Kibuya Parishes,
by Distance from Kampala's Western Boundary, 1957

Parish and Distance from Boundary	Average Size of Customary Holding
Parish A 1 Mile from Kampala Boundary	1/5 to 1/4 acre
Parish B 2 Miles from Kampala Boundary	1/3 to 1/2 acre
Parish C 3 Miles from Kampala Boundary	1 to 1-1/4 acres
Parish D 3-1/2 Miles from Kampala Boundary	3 to 3-1/2 acres

Source: P. C. W. Gutkind, *The Royal Capital of Buganda* (The Hague: Mouton and Company, 1963), p. 180.

Other groups benefiting from the new sources of income have found economic strength and thus a basis for a voice in government and the economy. Thus, while the landlord and plot holder represent in the urban environment the traditional African reverence for the land and through these interests find themselves involved in urban affairs, they are not in a position to dominate the shopkeepers, tradesmen, wage earners, and professional people whose incomes are mostly from employment and not land ownership. Associations of businessmen and labor unions reflect the emergence of these new groups.

CONCLUSION

We have dwelt at length upon the social structure and its changes in an African urban environment. These African urban worlds are quite different from the urban centers designed and developed largely by colonial governments. Such cities as Salisbury and Nairobi provide little insight into the processes of African urbanization and development. In approaching the problems of economic development, we plead for a reformulation of developmental theory that takes into account the nature of traditional societies and the constructive role which they of necessity must play. Development theory requires more than a begrudging inclusion of social factors, such as the role of cities incorporated into the work of Bert Hoselitz,[34] or population growth as included in the work of Leibenstein,[35] or preconditions in the form of an ethic of hard work and austere living, which are emphasized in the writing of Barbara Ward.[36]

The theories of economic growth according to stages, though instructive, have been modeled on European and American economic history, and have carried the implication that a Protestant ethic, or its equivalent, is an essential precondition

---

[34] Bert F. Hoselitz, *Sociological Aspects of Economic Growth* (Glencoe: The Free Press, 1960).
[35] Harvey Leibenstein, *Economic Backwardness and Economic Growth* (New York: John Wiley & Sons, 1963).
[36] Barbara Ward, *The Rich Nations and the Poor Nations* (New York: Norton, 1962).

Indeed, every economy will operate and develop within an ethic which provides a motivation for work and an evaluation of ends, but this ethic does not have to be imported, nor can it be transmitted as a part of foreign aid.

Emile Durkheim observed that, "A society can neither create itself nor recreate itself without at the same time creating an ideal."[37] That the foreigner often does not recognize these ideals is not argument that they do not exist. Everyone who has tried to administer a program of foreign aid has finally had to admit that what can be brought from outside a society is infinitely less significant for that society's development than what springs from within. It is more realistic to think of development growing out of the traditional society rather than apart from it and in opposition to it. Every traditional society has built up a large reservoir of values, motivations, and arrangements which provide security, solace, and the driving force which is needed to recreate itself as a more adequate society.

We have shown that Africans are coming increasingly to live and work in towns, that they save for investments on the land and in education. Their motivation in the new social world is nurtured in the old. The traditional values of land, space, peace, security and family may not be sufficient to orient and generate a capitalistic economy like those in the East; but surely these traditional values are adequate ends in terms of which an African economy may be rationally and effectively constructed. Such ends always have the advantage over imported ethics in that they are deep-seated, authentic, active, and therefore most likely to provide an adequate motivation for the enormous effort required to develop a modern economy. Africans may appropriate ideas and adapt technologies from everywhere; but in the fundamental drive to achieve, the African economies must be thoroughly African, for therein lies their best opportunity for advance.

---

[37] Emile Durkheim, *The Elementary Forms of the Religious Life* (Glencoe: The Free Press, 1954), p. 422.

CHAPTER **5** THE DEVELOPMENT OF TRADE UNIONS IN NEW NATIONS

Arnold M. Zack[†]

During the past decade, the role of trade unions in Africa has undergone considerable adjustment because of the changing political environment in which they operate. Any effort at determining the ideal role for trade unions in Africa today, therefore, must first take into account the role labor has played since these nations achieved independence.

LABOR'S POSTINDEPENDENCE ROLE

During the colonial period, the trade unions appeared destined to play an important role after independence. A formidable force in the struggle for independence, the labor movement was logically expected to be equally important in the postindependence period. Moving beyond mere representation of the organized labor force, the trade unions were frequently visualized also as important elements in the formation of national development policy once independence was achieved, and in implementing the

---

[†]Arnold M. Zack is President of International Manpower Development, Inc. As a manpower and labor economics specialist, he has been a consultant to the U.S. Department of Labor, USAID, the U.S. Peace Corps, the Ethiopian Government, the Friedrich-Ebert Stiftung and the OECD. Lecturer on labor economics at Haile Selassie University from 1963 to 1965, he is the author of *Labor Training in Developing Countries* (1964); *Ethiopia's High Level Manpower* (1964); and a contributor to *Africa Handbook* (1966).

policy once it was formed.

Recognized for the important role they often had played in achieving national independence, in fact, a number of African labor leaders assumed new and important functions in the independent governments. Ironically, however, the political influence of the trade unions themselves was drastically reduced in the new states. In part, of course, the fault lay with the labor leaders themselves. For while they retained their union positions, frequently they had also taken on a much broader responsibility. Indeed, most of their constituents were now nonunion elements of the population since, at best, organized labor represented between 5/10 per cent of the total population. Diverting the attention of the labor/government official, the new demands tended naturally to downgrade labor interests. In other instances, even though they severed formal ties with the trade unions, ex-trade union leaders in government continued to maintain control of the labor movement they once had headed. However, instead of leading the movement, they now used it for their own political interests.

An obviously effective political force prior to independence, the labor movements posed serious problems in a number of the newly independent nations, particularly as one-party systems developed. For uncontrolled by the party, the labor movement naturally constituted a potential rallying point against it. Using tactics that are now well documented, therefore, the one-party system in a number of African states has been able gradually to undermine and finally destroy trade union autonomy entirely. Involving labor leaders in affairs of the party and government, the party diverts the attention of union leaders; providing buildings and financial support to the labor movements, the party subordinates the movement logistically to the party; substituting legislation in the name of national development for traditional union methods to achieve labor's goals, the party emasculates the labor movement of its very reason for existing; and, of particular interest, the party finally severs the movement's ties with fraternal international organizations that might be able to assist the movement to maintain or regain its autonomy.

THE QUESTION OF TRADE UNION AUTONOMY

This chapter is predicated on two basic and generally accepted assumptions: That (1) labor unions are essential for the improvement of the lot of the workers, and that (2) as mass-based democratic institutions, their continued existence is essential to democratic nation-building. However, having lost their leaders, their autonomy and, indeed, sometimes their very *raison d'être*, a number of African labor movements obviously do not measure up to these basic standards.

Attempts at strengthening the autonomy of African trade unions obviously connote a resurrection of their political independence and thus their potential threat to the government. Efforts along this line in African nations in which labor is patently suspect, therefore, are doomed to failure. Realistically speaking, the governments are the basic factor to consider within the African context. That they will concede autonomy to the labor movements, of course, is indeed remote.

If attempts at restoring trade union autonomy are doomed to failure, is there any other course of action which might still make the unions effective democratic institutions serving the interests of the workers in particular and the nation in general? Even where permitted, organizational and financial assistance from trade unions abroad is unlikely to prove effective. For as the local trade unions again begin to flex their muscles, they will merely incur further governmental controls.

Within this realistic framework, trade union development along democratic lines appears relatively improbable. Yet, there is one feasible approach which, fortunately, should also enjoy at least the government's acquiescence and perhaps even its endorsement. While it does not meet all the criteria of free trade unionism, this approach deserves at least consideration.

ALTERNATIVE UNION PROGRAMS IN NEW NATIONS

In essence, trade union programs should concentrate on

the economic and social spheres. On the one hand, these programs preserve the union objective of improving the conditions of the workers and, on the other, they coincide with the government's goals for national development. Serving mutual interests of labor and government, these programs also permit trade union development, since the labor movement will exercise at least a degree of control over the programs. While giving evidence of good faith in the program of national development, labor may also be able to serve its own interests in the traditional areas that deal with wages and conditions of employment.

PARTICIPATION IN NATIONAL PLANNING

Alleging that strong trade unions constitute an obstacle to national development plans, governments hesitate to call upon them to participate in planning. Yet, labor's participation would assist the government considerably in planning that concerns the wage-earning sector. Also, it would tend to weight properly the varying interest groups that assert pressures in the planning process. Participation in the planning process, of course, would also tend to rally worker support to at least those portions of the plan that are consonant with labor's own goals.

To exploit this new avenue of trade union activity, however, the unions must in a sense retool. The level of labor's understanding of the planning concept and its implementation, for example, must be raised through intensive training. In fact, this is the crux of the problem of trade union development in many of the new nations, since few movements can themselves provide the training. They require outside assistance. While the governments object to outside assistance of their labor movements within the traditional framework, they should logically concur in this form of assistance.

SKILL DEVELOPMENT

A second area in which the trade unions can provide for the needs the members have and, at the same time, strengthen their own position in the country as well as improve their image in the eyes of the government, is in providing skill training to the labor force. In effect, the trade unions will provide the skill training needs that are either implicit or are written in the national development programs. While contributing to the national effort, of course, the trade unions will also improve the earning capacity of their members.

Working with local employers who either share a sense of responsibility for the expansion of skills or who are themselves in need of workers with critical skills, the unions could develop effective skill training programs. The probability of this sort of arrangement developing, however, is unlikely within the immediate future of many new nations. In large measure, therefore, the task is essentially one that the labor unions would have to assume on their own. Requiring both financing and technical capabilities that most of the labor movements and, in fact, new nations themselves do not possess, these programs will again require outside assistance.

COOPERATIVES, HOUSING AND HEALTH PROGRAMS

Cooperatives represent more of a social than economic orientation. Thus, while the governments do not necessarily promote them as part of the central plan, they still welcome them to the extent that they contribute to economic development. Production cooperatives in particular should be attractive within this framework. Trade union involvement in cooperatives, of course, has not been developed to the extent that it should be in the new nations. The advantages accruing to the union members are obvious.

In the field of workers' housing, the cooperative concept can again be applied with telling effectiveness. Improving, on the one hand, the health and well-being of workers and their families, workers' housing programs also help, on the other hand, to stabilize the work force and thus to integrate it more closely into national development. Further in the interest of national economic development, housing cooperatives tend to encourage workers to invest their own savings in housing, which is generally acknowledged to be a high priority item in most developing countries.

Workers' health is another field which, while ignored for the most part to date, is ideal for trade union development. While few employers provide even minimal standard clinics for their workers, even the governments in most African countries have been unable to keep pace with the health needs of the rapidly urbanizing areas. Receiving little or no treatment for even the most easily controlled medical problems such as malaria, schistosomiasis, typhoid or viral infections, the workers are unable to contribute their full energies to their employment and thus to national development. Union-sponsored programs in health education and clinics to treat common ailments of union members and their families would constitute a dramatic contribution to the resolution of the general problem. Designed to provide only minimal medical treatment, the clinics could be located at union offices or, perhaps more effectively, in mobile units that move throughout the areas in which the unions operate.

Adding these suggested activities to the traditional programs of literacy training, adult education, women's and youth programs, as well as trade union training programs, the trade unions will quite probably evoke from African governments a positive instead of the negative response they had generated earlier.

IMPLEMENTING ALTERNATIVE PROGRAMS

Obviously the mounting of any one of the programs outlined briefly above entails resources far beyond the command of the individual African labor movement. Nevertheless, that the African labor movement itself originate the proposals, being careful to place them within the context of national development, is of paramount importance in generating both endorsement and support. For once the labor movement has won the government's endorsement, of course, it has a fair chance of winning support for the programs, either from the government itself and the employers or from fraternal organizations and private sources (foundations and so on) on the outside.

As for training union members for participation in the national planning process, for example, or for participation on tripartite panels that deal with labor problems within the national economy, obviously the government itself could well provide experts to lecture on these subjects before select trade union groups. In view of the similar stake that both the government and the employers have in vocational training and health clinics, the unions should also press for the complete support of sites for clinics, teachers and equipment, and should settle for no less than joint support.

Only when the employers and the government are either unwilling or unable to assume whole or partial support should an appeal be made for outside assistance. On the other hand, one must keep in mind that up to the present, program development in the African labor field has clearly demonstrated the need of external assistance.

The International Confederation of Free Trade Unions (ICFTU), the International Trade Secretariats (ITS) and many national labor movements have promised to support African trade unions in their economic and social programs. So far, however, the concrete execution of these promises has been limited. Indeed, to mount programs that will have a meaningful impact on the society, one must think in terms of a broad spectrum coverage, permanent organizations and, of course, coordinated implementation of the programs themselves. Since programs of this magnitude are almost prohibitively expensive to mount, obviously most national labor movements can provide only limited assistance to their African counterparts.

While backed by the powerful AFL-CIO, the African-American Labor Center established in New York is a case in point. It has plans in various stages of development for technical material assistance to African labor movements, for example, in most of the areas outlined above. Nevertheless, there is a need for coordinated planning and cooperative operations as other national centers also involve themselves in similar assistance programs. But even with the ultimate in participation of other national labor movements, their coordinated efforts face an enormous task, which indeed may be beyond the capabilities of even the entire international trade union movement.

Government assistance from donor countries through their trade union movements is an obvious answer to the financial problem. But this in turn raises questions regarding programming and policies, both in the donor country and in the recipient state. In fact, this approach poses all the problems, practical and ideological, that have marked all assistance programs since World War II.

The fact remains that attention must be devoted to finding sources other than the labor movements for financing, teaching personnel, training equipment, administrative assistance and so on. Following the lead of the United States, other nations have also developed their own peace corps which, it has been found, are particularly adept at vocational training and could, perhaps, also provide training in developing planning. Retired businessmen's groups, religious organizations, youth groups, cooperative societies, charitable organizations and others might also be enlisted in the tasks outlined earlier. Out of interest in promoting and establishing their products in the new nations, it is possible that some corporations would also be willing to provide equipment for training purposes.

There is an unreasoned reluctance of too many private foundations and semigovernmental organizations and institutions to become "involved" with the trade unions of the developing nations. This fear of identification with the trade union movement stems from their being identified as a "negative political force" in Africa during the past few years. But it is exactly this image that must be changed. The unions must, in fact, do a public relations job of great magnitude, not only in their own countries but abroad as well. They must convince private and governmental institutions that African trade unions, beyond being merely essential protectors of the rights of workers, are fundamental to the type of democratic national development that they themselves envision for Africa.

CONCLUSION

If the programs outlined above can be implemented, the African labor movements will have taken a major step in re-establishing themselves with their governments. Indeed, they apparently have no other alternative except to wither away completely. On the other hand, they can continue to operate within this framework and, indeed, may eventually achieve again the autonomy that many feel is truly essential to nation-building.

CHAPTER 6 NATION-BUILDING AND
THE INTERNATIONAL FREE
TRADE UNION MOVEMENT

Daniel C. Lazorchick and Charles R. Hare[†]

"The future of the world is not governed by blind destiny: it has been placed under our control. We have the power to study and consider the facts and translate our ideals into action."[1] These words of Gunnar Myrdal are apt words for a conference on the role of labor in nation-building. They reflect what reason tells each of us--that man need not be the helpless victim of circumstances if he chooses to pursue actively another course. And secondly, they project a sensible and admirable goal; namely, the study and consideration of acts with a view to translating ideals into action.

No perceptive observer of developments in Africa during the last eight years has any uncertainty about how the leaders of that continent view the future. Their fierce determination and resolve to achieve for their peoples a radically improved and different existence against formidable economic obstacles must be manifestly clear. If one accepts the premise that nothing great has ever been accomplished without enthusiasm, this determination is comforting to behold, because the populace

---

[†]Daniel C. Lazorchick is Chief of the Division of International Trade Union Organizations, Bureau of International Labor Affairs, U.S. Department of Labor. He is the author of *The Miners' International Federation* (1962). Charles R. Hare is International Relations Officer in the Division of International Trade Union Organizations, Bureau of International Labor Affairs, U.S. Department of Labor. The views expressed here are those of the authors and should in no way be construed as reflecting official policy of the U.S. Government or of the U.S. Department of Labor.

[1]The quotation is taken from L. J. Lebret, *The Last Revolution*, translated by John Horgan (New York: Sheed and Ward, 1965), p. 3.

of Africa desperately needs and deserves nothing less.

Yet determination in this situation is only the propellant, and therefore only part of the requirement. More important are the honest study and consideration of facts and the firm resolve that whatever action results reflects ideals as well as expediency.

These observations are strikingly relevant for African trade unionism, which today is undergoing the agonizing process of attempting to fashion for itself a meaningful yet acceptable role in societies generally skeptical and uneasy about the role unions should play. As Professor Windmuller of Cornell University has written,

> The requirements of nation-building and forced-draft development, as interpreted by most African governments, have left too small a margin for the toleration of labor organizations free to set their own tasks... Although the situation varies from country to country and is subject to mercurial changes within any one country, the independence and strength of trade unions in Africa have in general diminished rather than increased, their ability to protect the more immediate interests of their members has been sharply circumscribed, their contribution to the development of political democracy has with some important exceptions been quite negligible, and their role in economic development schemes remains to be defined, if by "role" something beyond the disciplining of the labor force is meant.[2]

This assessment of African trade unionism, scrupulously accurate, should give pause to all thinking Africans, and all true friends of Africa, as much for what it implies as for what it conveys explicitly. Given the enormous needs for improvement in the living and working conditions of the great bulk of the population in every country on the continent, and the scarce human and material resources available to effect this improvement, this assessment makes clear that to an important degree resources are being wasted and opportunities missed.

---

[2] John P. Windmuller, "Cohesion and Disunity in the ICFTU: The 1965 Amsterdam Congress," *Industrial and Labor Relations Review*, Vol. XIX, No.3 (April, 1966), pp. 362-63

"Nation-building" can be a deceptive expression if it is taken to mean simply developing a country's economy in the direction of viability. Important as this consideration is, it represents no more than an important first step in the process of creating a meaningful society for the peoples found within a particular set of geographical boundaries. Indeed, it covers the growth in the production of goods and services within a country, but what of the other values in life, many of which are nonmaterial? It is with this latter consideration in mind that we wish to scrutinize developments in the trade union field in Africa today.

GOVERNMENT ATTITUDES TOWARD TRADE UNIONS

Allowing for minor deviations in some particulars, most African governments look upon their respective trade union movements as organized segments of society to be continuously watched and carefully held in check. In many instances among the best organized and disciplined mass movements within the society, the unions are considered "special pleaders" whose principal aim is to obtain more and more in wages, improved working conditions, and other benefits and amenities for the organized work force, which in Africa rarely exceeds 10 per cent of the total working population. In these terms, to give unions a free reign to pursue their narrow objectives is visibly to sanction an ever-widening income gap between those workers organized into trade unions and those in the nonunion ranks of the work force. Apart from the economic costs of such a policy in countries pressing for capital accumulation at the greatest possible rate, such a policy contains implications for domestic politics too substantial for most governments to treat lightly.

African governments, for the most part under single party rule, have manifested a reluctance to permit the existence of autonomous centers of power which obviously represent potential if not actual sources of opposition. Experience in Africa and elsewhere during recent years indicates this fear is not unfounded. Coups or attempted coups involving trade unions in Tanzania, Congo (Brazzaville), Dahomey, Burundi and the Sudan contained lessons not lost on other African governments. An observable result has been that the actions of most African governments in promptly suppressing any behavior on the part of unions resembling general unrest reveal an excessive nervousness about the threat such behavior represents for them. Frequently the outside observer is struck by the prompt quashing by African governments of what appear to be politically innocent disturbances in the industrial relations field.

Perhaps of equal importance is the concern of governments that, if given a relatively free hand, trade unions will in effect sabotage economic development programs through their unceasing pressure for higher wages and improved working conditions for those they represent. Working against formidable economic odds, African governments generally have shown themselves intolerant of any trade union activity which can be interpreted as threatening to shut down production facilities, or possibly triggering inflationary pressures, and in that way damaging efforts to achieve economic advance as rapidly as possible at the least possible cost in terms of scarce financial and manpower resources.

Related to this is the fact that roughly 35 per cent of the organized workers on the African continent are engaged in what might broadly be characterized as industries in the public service field: transport, communications, civil service, etc. As the employers of the largest single segment of organized workers in their countries, African governments are highly sensitive to trade union demands emanating from that field, both because such demands might readily be interpreted as motivated by groups desirous of embarrassing the governments in power, and because of the pattern-setting nature of governmental decisions in the industrial relations field. If governments are to be effective in restraining wage demands, perforce they must take the lead in demonstrating how this must be done with respect to their own employees. Further, every wage increase granted by a government reduces by the aggregate amount the funds it can devote to economic development projects for the benefit of the country as a whole.

With respect to the private sector, African governments also have a vested interest in keeping wages in line, since any imbalance in favor of the private sector will create pressures for wage increases in public employment. In addition, governments which are attempting to attract foreign investment want to maintain reasonably attractive wage levels for potential investors.

AFRICAN TRADE UNION FUNCTIONS

For all the foregoing reasons, most African governments increasingly have felt compelled to establish firm control over the trade union movements either by legislative action or by intervention. This has resulted in a considerable diminution of the traditional function of unions as collective bargaining agents. Nevertheless, most governments continue to envision a narrow role in the economic development process for the trade union movement; i.e., as a vehicle for mobilizing and disciplining the work force and increasing productivity. African governments also are beginning to recognize the potential of unions as orderly channels for worker discontent and even as important social institutions for the urbanized worker who no longer enjoys the communal advantages of the tribal society.

It is argued that by undertaking and fulfilling these functions, the trade union movement no longer remains an adversary of the government but becomes a partner in the development process. However, the best will in the world on the part of the trade union leaders will not necessarily assure effective performance in this role. Much depends on the rank-and-file membership, which can be expected to respect and follow the union leadership only so long as it is convinced that such leadership produces concrete benefits.

PROCESSING WORKER GRIEVANCES

However "inconvenient" indigenous trade unions might be in the eyes of African governments, experience demonstrates that in this age, workers, whether organized or not, can be counted upon to find an effective means of protest whenever they feel deeply about their terms of employment, condition in society as a group, or treatment as human beings with dignity and worth. Whatever the geographical entity, when the feeling of despair and dissatisfaction among workers becomes intense, we witness spontaneous outbreaks of protest, sometimes orderly but often violent in proportion to the intensity of the feeling of discontent pervading those protesting. Where these workers are leaderless, at least at the outset, their very presence in large numbers in a factory or on a plantation provides an environment inviting group action. Protest in these circumstances can be most awkward because it is unpredictable, uncontrollable and often unreasoning.

One of the benefits of responsible unions in any society is that they provide an effective vehicle for processing worker grievances and, therefore, a means through which the more damaging manifestations of worker protest--halting production, destroying property, and committing other acts of physical destruction--often can be avoided. Similarly, such unions provide a valuable channel for the dissemination of information, ideas and policies to the rank and file comprising the membership.

BARGAINING IN THE PRIVATE SECTOR

Throughout Africa a substantial amount of economic activity falls within the jurisdiction of the private sector. Historically, this has been the area of greatest trade union activity in the traditional sense. Currently, with governments hypersensitive to any developments capable of triggering inflationary pressures, wage claims and other demands by unions active in the private sector have brought sharp reactions from the governments concerned. Though perhaps absolutely necessary in some instances, it can be argued that as a general policy, this practice has serious limitations and therefore deserves to be reviewed critically.

No amount of wishing otherwise can alter the fact that trade unions do exist in Africa and trade unionism and its functions are known to millions of African workers. Many of these workers also know of the activities and achievements of trade unions elsewhere in the world. If they honestly do not expect of their unions all they know unions abroad have achieved for their membership, most certainly they cannot be persuaded to think their own unions are fulfilling a meaningful role for them when that clearly is not the case.

If unions in Africa perform only those roles permitted by governments, then as Professor Eliot Berg of Harvard properly observed, "erosion or total loss of the *bona fides* of the trade unions in Communist countries is persuasive in this regard: the unions there tend to be ignored by the workers, who seek other channels to express dissent and dissatisfaction."[3]

It would appear to be in the private sector that within carefully drawn limits, African governments could best tolerate the performance of some of the traditional functions by indigenous unions; i.e., negotiating with the employers over conditions of employment, which include hours of work, sick leave, paid holidays, retirement annuities, safety regulations, and even wage rates, to an extent short of setting in motion disastrous inflationary forces.

Unpalatable as this might sound on first reading to governments committed to rapid economic development, the ultimate results of a contrary policy would appear upon reflection to be infinitely more unappealing. Granted that firm control of the trade union movement may reduce to a minimum the possibilities for work stoppages as long as this control is effectively maintained; nevertheless, what the economy gains in wage stability and uninterrupted production under such conditions could easily be more than offset by widespread passive resistance and disinterest among workers with the resultant loss in productivity. And this is not to mention the possibility that stifled worker protest could eventually lead to worker collaboration in an uprising against the government when the opportunity for revolt occurs, as in the Sudan in October, 1964. In fact it may be argued that African governments have more to gain than lose in the long run by tolerating relatively free trade unionism of the traditional pattern if, at the same time, they encourage their union movements to join as partners in the nation-building efforts by enlarging their range of activities to include undertakings commonly considered in the social projects domain. In the last analysis, concessions on matters falling within the traditional trade union sphere might well be the price African governments will be obliged to pay to attain the stability and worker cooperation without which economic development schemes will founder.

But another consideration should not be overlooked. That is the moral consideration of equity. An inherent danger in forced-draft economic development of the type characteristic in the developing countries today is that in the highly specialized business of establishing priorities and striking neat balances in

---

[3]Unpublished paper entitled, "African Labor Movement," May, 1965, p. 67.

the allocation of scarce resources, the ultimate objective of the whole undertaking, namely the improvement of the condition of life of the country's inhabitants in the fullest sense, can be easily lost to view as the managing of economic forces becomes an all-consuming passion and an end in itself. As a result, "things" rather than "people" determine priorities, with the consequence that the gratification of the basic needs and desires of the masses is postponed and placed lower and lower on the scale of the country's schedule of goals in the interest of the fulfillment of the development plan. Often, when this occurs, entrepreneurial and other elites in the society are not similarly disadvantaged. The social and political implications of this development need no elaboration.

Experience demonstrates that workers, individually and as a group, are fully prepared to make sacrifices so long as they have the feeling that all segments of society likewise are making sacrifices for patriotic purposes. It is, not surprisingly, another matter where they detect an inequality of sacrifice, even if it involves only those holding high political office.

Beyond that, there would appear to be no overriding reason why economic planning should not have built into it an improvement factor for all members of society, so that all represented in the "present generation" benefit in some direct and recognizable economic way at the same time the nation-building process is under way. This would necessarily mean the pace of economic advance would be deliberately scaled back to compensate for this programmed distribution of benefits; but is it not only fair that those counted upon to produce the goods and services of society enjoy during their lifetime some of the fruits of their toil in the form of at least some improvement in their condition of life?

PROVIDING SOCIAL SERVICES

Considering the present trend in collective bargaining, if the African trade union movement is to succeed in its new and not yet clearly defined role, we feel that in addition to fulfilling its traditional functions, at least in part, the unions inevitably must run more and more toward social projects which provide measurable benefits to the membership without detracting from government economic development programs. In fact, these socially and economically useful union activities should complement government efforts at nation-building.

It is outside the scope of this chapter to deal at length with the various types of projects that unions in Africa might undertake to the advantage of their nations as well as their membership, but among them should be: vocational training and skill-improvement programs, literacy training, adult education, establishment of credit unions and cooperatives, the institution of modest worker housing schemes, operation of health clinics, and the introduction of programs both to help workers adapt to industrial life and to gain an appreciation of the dignity of manual labor.

One other point should be mentioned at this juncture. The trade union movement can hardly be expected to function as a partner, however junior, in the development process without being involved directly in the planning of the economic development program. The form its involvement will take must, of necessity, vary from country to country, depending on political party-trade union relationships and the various governmental bodies engaged in planning and economic and social decision-making. The substance of its involvement, on the other hand, will depend almost entirely on its capacity to make available highly trained and talented representatives who will be accorded respect by those with whom they serve because of their abilities rather than because of the organizations with which they are identified. Let there be no illusions on this point. To repeat, if the trade unions are to exercise a real voice in economic development planning, they must have research specialists and economists whose skills equal or excel those of the other participants in the planning process.

In examining African trade union movements today, one observes that to a limited extent, social projects already have become a part of trade union action programs in some countries, although the pattern varies widely and most of the projects are limited in scope. Notwithstanding this development, with few exceptions the trade unions of Africa are not in a position to mount on their own the broad-gauged, comprehensive and varied programs required of them if they are to make a significant contribution to the changing African society. Most of the leaders and staffs of these organizations have been schooled and trained in the traditional trade union tasks of organizing and collective bargaining. Accordingly, the unions will need to develop or acquire cadres of administrative and technical specialists to perform the new tasks.

With the exception of those few trade union organizations which enjoy both relatively large memberships and effective dues check-off arrangements, most unions in Africa lack the resources to finance the new activities, and most are without the trained specialists to implement them effectively, if indeed the necessary funds were available. Viewed realistically, there would appear to be little justification for the conclusion that the African unions can resolve this dilemma without assistance from beyond continental boundaries.

INTERNATIONAL TRADE UNION INVOLVEMENT

The international free trade union movement,[4] not unnaturally, has suffered keen disappointment over recent trends in trade union development in Africa. However, of late there have been indications that it is engaged in a fresh assessment of the African trade union situation which recognizes that initial expectations for rapid and significant trade union development prevalent in the immediate postindependence period were not founded on a realistic appraisal of the economic and political conditions operative in Africa. While the basic concepts and procedures of free trade unionism initially found a fertile field on that continent, since independence it has become obvious that these same ideas and methods would have to be remolded to fit circumstances markedly different from those of the colonial era.

Given the traditions and deeply ingrained precepts of the international free trade union movement, it understandably has not been an easy matter for the unions comprising that movement to adapt their methods and practices to economic cir-

---

[4]The expression "international free trade union movement" is used here to designate collectively those international trade union organizations which are composed of trade union federations and confederations in countries comprising the free world: International Confederation of Free Trade Unions (ICFTU), International Federation of Christian Trade Unions (CISC), and the nineteen International Trade Secretariats; e.g., Transport Workers (ITF), Metalworkers (IMF), Miners (MIF) and Commercial Workers (IFCCTE).

cumstances strikingly different from those in which they function, or to accept the fact that political circumstances in Africa would not permit there the freedom of action they successfully fought for and jealously guard in their home countries.

Yet, clearly, adaptation to these circumstances is taking place, though more slowly in some cases than others, owing largely to the fact that some unions have been more assiduous than others in gaining an understanding of the essential differences between the societies of the developed and the developing areas of the world.

One of the factors responsible for facilitating the adaptation process in important ways is the spirit of international solidarity which historically has accounted in large measure for the interest that unions of the free world and the international trade union organizations with which they are affiliated have shown toward unions in Africa. This interest, especially apparent in the early 1950's, is much maligned and often grossly misunderstood. Those with ideological axes to grind deliberately ascribe to it motivation and purposes which do not survive the test of critical examination.

For almost a century, organized workers of almost all nations permitting trade unions to exist have maintained and nourished bonds of amity and friendship with one another through their respective unions, under the banner of worker solidarity. Generated originally among those in Europe sharing a fervent faith in the principles and ultimate triumph of socialism, this worker solidarity has had its most virulent expression and therefore its brightest moments on those occasions when, for those involved, the economic stakes were immediate and high. The chronicle containing detailed accounts of manifestations of worker solidarity across national boundaries over such issues as tariffs, other trade policies, strikes with international implications, and minimum-hours legislation, among other matters, not only makes fascinating reading but readily establishes the authenticity and deep-seated character of this spirit of worker kinship.

In the idiom of the prize ring, despite the heavy body blows it absorbed during the two world wars in its bouts with political nationalism, this spirit of brotherhood among workers regardless of race, religion or national origin, survived and persists vibrant and dynamic today.

The cynical identify it as a naive belief among the unlettered working classes that worker solidarity around the world might one day spell the difference between survival or destruction of the human race. A more objective evaluation identifies it as a genuine kinship among workers arising out of their common experience, often bitter, contesting with oppressive employers and pressuring governments for improved wages and conditions of work, protective labor legislation, and the other amenities related to an acceptable level of living and the dignity of the individual.

This kinship understandably is strongest across national boundaries among working men and women of the same industry or trade--railwaymen, miners, metalworkers, communications workers, and printers, to name a few. In addition to its firm basis in self-interest, it is characterized by strong humanitarian proclivities, most often surprising to those who observe its full measure for the first time. But the latter trait is by no means a new or recent phenomenon. Like some other characteristics of the international free trade union movement, it has an unbroken history dating to the 1860's, and represents one of the more remarkable aspects of this movement, whose history regrettably is less well known by the political elite of Africa than by the trade union leadership of that continent.

It is against this backdrop that one must view international trade union activity on the part of free unions in Africa today. More than any other factor, the humanitarian element accounts for the considerable human and material resources put to work there in the service of trade unionism. In addition, this activity is mounted by many independent organizations usually responding individually to observed needs or requests from kindred African unions. Above all, it is motivated genuinely by trade union interests, as distinct from governmental or employer pressures, as its detractors delight in alleging. Who denies this and believes what he says, understands the subject hardly at all. Thus it is that one should expect such activity to continue as long as there exists a feeling of brotherhood among workers of two or more countries, particularly among workers of the same industries or trades.

In important respects this worker solidarity springs from the same emotional roots in humanity which, for example, cause political leaders and citizens of various countries--African and non-African alike--to make financial and other sacrifices to combat apartheid in the Republic of South Africa, minority white control in Rhodesia, and Portuguese rule in Angola and Mozambique. These are sacrifices more of the heart than the head, and in that way differ not a whit from those currently being made by the international free trade union movement in Africa, notwithstanding the characterization of the latter by critics as "neocolonialist" or "imperialist." Unless the actions are understood in these terms, they are understood not at all, and perhaps worse, the organizations responsible for them are neither fairly judged nor sufficiently comprehended to be of service where their contributions can be of great value.

INTERNATIONAL TRADE UNION ASSISTANCE

If some African politicians have interpreted the activities of the international free trade union movement in sinister and conspiratorial terms, many surprisingly also have failed to see the indirect benefits to African societies of association of indigenous unions with trade union organizations of the free world. In almost all instances, these associations are with unions which, within their respective countries, represent important numbers of voters and therefore are politically important individually, and even more so when affiliated nationally with a powerful trade union national center. As such, often they exercise considerable influence on their governments, even to the extent of initiating and securing passage of favored legislation. As illustrated in the United States by major domestic legislation adopted this year and by successive foreign assistance acts, significant programs of a government thus are susceptible to influence exerted directly or indirectly by a powerful trade union movement in ways that movement's leadership considers appropriate. Hence, one finds numerous instances wherein governmental action at both legislative and executive levels has been shaped, modified, or on occasion blocked by trade union forces whose power is too great to be ignored by those holding political office.

The lesson for Africa to be drawn from the foregoing is that the association of African unions with their counterparts in the free world should be viewed in the broadest of contexts. Immediately observable are the results of that association in trade union terms, ranging from the exchange of fraternal delegations to programs of technical and financial assistance for

strictly trade union purposes. Less apparent but no less real--
and perhaps of more far-reaching significance--are the indirect
results of such association as reflected, among other ways, in
governmental attitudes and programs in the field of foreign affairs.
It would indeed be uncommonly strange if in those societies
where trade unions are influential, their preferences were
not reflected in the foreign as well as domestic programs and
attitudes of the governments in power.

African trade union movements have long enjoyed access
to considerable technical and financial assistance from their
counterparts in the developed countries, either directly or
through the latter's respective international organizations.
Among the unions in the developed countries can be found the
technical skills required for the various types of social projects
envisioned for African trade unions. The unions in the
industrialized countries also can marshal the requisite financial
resources to fund union participation in the broad social
development program desperately needed in Africa. In the
past, trade unions in the developed countries have demonstrated
their willingness to commit substantial human and material
resources to aid in the formation and development of trade
unions in Africa. It would be surprising if these same unions
were not now equally prepared to assist their African counterparts
at a time when their support is more needed than ever
before.

The present and projected activities of the organizations
currently assisting African unions clearly indicate that the
international free trade union movement is moving slowly but
steadily in the direction of making available the type of aid
being sought by African unions for the new programs required
by the present situation.

THE CHALLENGE

All of this portends the evolution and development of a
productive and necessary three-way relationship between African
governments, African trade unions and the international
free trade union movement. The prevailing circumstances demand
nothing less. Hopefully, the parties involved, after an

honest and tough-minded review of the facts, will cast aside suspicions and distrusts harbored from the past and work together for the objectives they share in common.

Obviously, this course of action, given the volatile ingredients present for each of the parties, calls for a high order of statesmanship and not a little bit of daring. No one here needs to be reminded of the explosive character of some of the issues at stake. On the part of the governments, perhaps overly sensitive to the development of any organizations which even remotely represent a prospective base of opposition, there are inherent political risks for anyone championing a course favoring collaboration with trade unions. Again for the governments, there is the question of welcoming collaboration with foreign or international trade union organizations at a time when throughout Africa, great suspicion exists concerning the reasons why such trade unions are prepared to make considerable financial and other contributions to assist counterpart unions on the African continent.

For the trade unions, collaboration with governments immediately poses the question of the ultimate consequences of such collaboration. Will it, among other things, mean that governments will move in where they have not already done so to make meaningful decisions for the trade unions? Or will it mean any eventual undoing of the trade union movement as illustrated by the rhyme about the lady from Niger who was enticed to ride on on the back of the tiger-- and completed her journey in the tiger's stomach?

For the international free trade union movement there is the large and important question of association in a common effort with governments which circumscribe trade union freedom to an extent normally unacceptable to unions in the free world. Despite the cynicism of some on this issue, the fact remains that the principle of freedom of association is a basic tenet of the free trade union movement. It continues today to retain much of its original force.

Yet, viewing these conditions against the circumstances prevailing in Africa today, the question arises as to whether the leaders of governments, indigenous unions and the international free trade union movement are prepared to forsake goals and objectives they honestly desire to achieve in favor of perpetuating a situation conditioned more by fear and emotionalism than by an honest and painstaking examination of the objective facts in the case. Again, for all parties concerned to brush aside the emotionally charged aspects of this situation in favor of attaining a higher plane of objectivity demands a degree of courage easier to accept in theory than to demonstrate in practice. Notwithstanding, such courage is called for in the present situation. We are convinced that the legitimate interests of all of Africa will be served grandly by an exhibition of this kind of courage now. What is at stake for Africa, in our judgment, is not failure or progress, but great progress as opposed to modest progress, and the release of energies making possible the exploitation of a galaxy of opportunities for the enrichment of the lives of all Africans.

PART III

LABOR'S ROLE IN
SUPRANATION-BUILDING

CHAPTER 7 LABOR: STUMBLING BLOCK
TO PAN-AFRICANISM

Dorothy Nelkin [†]

Pan-Africanism has been a dynamic and compelling concept throughout the continent for many years, but its embodiment in viable continental institutions has had only limited success. While the formation of the Organization of African Unity (OAU) has formally dissolved regional political groupings, this has been accomplished only by avoiding many of the concrete issues that would serve to upset its tenuous position. While sustained by its ideological basis, Pan-Africanism is confronted with a reality on the continent today which works against its institutionalization. Nowhere has this been more evident than in the sphere of labor, where continental trade union organization has been regarded as an instrument or building block to ultimate political Pan-Africanism.

> Considering that cooperation amongst African States in the social and labor fields is vital and will contribute to the reality of a sound solidarity... a committee of experts is called... to lay down a program ... to strengthen inter-African cooperation through the establishment of an African Trade Union.[1]

[†]Dorothy Nelkin is a Research Associate at the New York State School of Industrial and Labor Relations, Cornell University. She contributed a chapter to William H. Friedland and Carl G. Rosberg, Jr. (eds.), *African Socialism* (Stanford: Stanford University Press, 1964) and wrote an article on continental trade union organizations in *Africa Report*, Vol. X, No. 6 (June, 1965).

[1]From the Supplementary Resolutions adopted by the Summit Conference of the Independent African States, Addis Ababa, Ethiopia, May, 1963.

The abortive attempts to establish an all-African trade union organization reflect the divisions which continue to exist in the political arena. Moreover, the problems which have impeded trade union unity point up the fact that the labor situation is a major obstacle to realizing the Pan-African ideal. The continental trade union groupings which have emerged are largely paper organizations operating on an ideological level that is often unrealistic. These organizations will be treated briefly, after which the analysis will turn to a consideration of those aspects intrinsic to the labor situation which obstruct continental agreement in the matter of trade union unity.

THE CONTINENTAL TRADE UNION ORGANIZATIONS

A superficial survey and review of the major events related to the organization of continental groups indicate the extent to which the commitment to Pan-Africanism has pervaded the labor movement. This has been strongly encouraged by both the trade union and the political leadership. Sekou Touré led the formation of the Union Générale des Travailleurs d'Afrique Noire (UGTAN) in French West Africa in early 1957 to "spearhead" the struggle for liberation, and he continued as its leading protagonist after moving into political leadership in Guinea. Kwamé Nkrumah has long been committed to the formation of an all-African trade union as a "dynamic and positive instrument in the realization of a United States of Africa."[2] Throughout the continent, the idea of an all-African trade union organization has always been welcomed with enthusiastic vocal support. However, as the initial issue of anticolonialism became less crucial, the efforts to implement this idea resulted in a state of affairs that mirrored the Casablanca-Monrovia split as it existed prior to the formation of the OAU.

Since 1962, there have existed three main continental trade union groupings, none of which is in any sense representative of total continental interests. These three groups are the All African Trade Union Federation (AATUF), the

---

[2]Kwamé Nkrumah, "Speech at the opening of the Hall of Trade Unions at Accra, July 9, 1960," in *Labour*, Vol. I, No. 2 (August, 1966), p. 25.

African Regional Organization (AFRO) of the International Confederation of Free Trade Unions (ICFTU), and the African Trade Union Confederation (ATUC). All agree on two points; first, that Pan-African unity is an ultimate goal, and second, that the role of trade unions is essentially political in the sense that it is tied to national development. But on the pragmatic level involving the tactics of organization, there are two distinct and incompatible approaches.

THE ALL AFRICAN TRADE UNION FEDERATION

The All African Trade Union Federation takes a revolutionary and militant stance, requiring a high degree of centralization and emphasizing uniformity among its constituents. Its goal ultimately is "to coordinate and direct the action of national trade union centers."[3] Moreover, AATUF's position implies a relation between unions and political parties that goes beyond the idea of institutional cooperation for the fulfillment of the common goal of national development. Unions, it is implied, are to be political auxiliaries rather than independent entities, although this has not necessarily been the case with all its affiliates.

In contrast, AFRO and ATUC take a more moderate and pragmatic approach emphasizing autonomy and diversity. These differences have become manifest largely in the issue of the right of national centers to affiliate with international organizations. AATUF has made disaffiliation from international organizations a prerequisite to the formation of a continental trade union organization. Encouraged by the Ghanaian Government, the organization reflects Nkrumah's militant position in the Pan-African movement. Ghanaian responsibility and continued influence over AATUF have in fact, been quite explicit:[4]

---

[3]Quoted from the Preamble of AATUF's Charter from the Conference in Bamako, June, 1964, in Colin Legum, *Pan-Africanism* (New York: Praeger, 1965), p. 91.
[4]Statement by John Tettegah in *Labour*, Vol. II, No. 10 (April, 1961), p. 15, quoted in Giles Robert Wright, II, *Pan Africanism and the Ghana TUC* (Thesis, Howard University, Washington, D.C., June 8, 1962), p. 74.

> We cannot forget that the Ghana Trade Union Congress is the first free trade union organization in the first independent Black African State and that we have a duty to assist those who are travelling that same path to freedom.

Beyond such statements, Ghanaian influence is evident in the leadership of John Tettegah, a member of the Central Committee of the Ghana Convention People's Party, who was primarily responsible for AATUF's highly centralized structure. The publication of the organization's newspaper in Accra and the transfer of the permanent headquarters to a building furnished by the Ghanaian Government in Accra in 1964, further indicate the Ghanaian role in AATUF.

While AATUF's membership has been growing, the significance of its growth is hard to assess. Its nucleus consists of the unions of the former Casablanca powers[5] plus the newly formed National Union of Tanganyika Workers and the Nigerian Trades Union Congress. Beyond these, AATUF has successfully encouraged disaffected groups from within national unions to create splinter organizations. The affiliation of these groups is important to AATUF in validating its claim to Pan-Africanism and in providing a potential channel of influence within various countries.

THE AFRICAN REGIONAL ORGANIZATION

AFRO, the regional organization of the ICFTU, was formed in November, 1959 and established as an autonomous grouping one year later. ICFTU concerns in Africa have been based on the principle that through financial, educational and advisory assistance, trade unionism in Africa would develop along the lines of Western models of free trade unionism, and this would ultimately have a long-range influence over general political and ideological commitments.

The policy of the ICFTU concerning the distribution of its African expenditures has varied, but the usual pattern has been

---

[5] Ghana, Guinea, Mali, Algeria, Morocco, United Arab Republic.

to channel support through national trade union centers. As the pressure for the creation of a continental trade union organization developed, the ICFTU began to concentrate its efforts increasingly on the Pan-African level through its regional machinery. This shift in emphasis has stemmed largely from the desire to countervail the influence of AATUF, rather than from the needs of the African trade union movement. Thus AFRO maintained a position on affiliation that was obviously in direct contrast to that of AATUF; namely, that national union centers be free to affiliate with international organizations.

AFRO has been losing support as African governments are increasingly encouraging disaffiliation. The extent of this loss is indicated by the following table:[6]

TABLE 15

Comparison of African ICFTU Affiliates
in 1962 and 1964

	1962	1964
Affiliation fees received from Africa.	$136,229	$58,049
No. of affiliated organizations[7]	30	14
African membership in ICFTU affiliated unions (approx.).	2,287,000	905,000

Despite such losses, however, the ICFTU continues its

---

[6]ICFTU, Eighth World Congress, Amsterdam, July, 1965, *Report on Activities and Financial Reports, 1962-1964* (Brussels: ICFTU, 1965), extracted from listings on pages 311, 338-43.

[7]Major changes, either through dissolution or disaffiliation have occurred in the following countries since 1962: Algeria, Chad, Congo-Brazzaville, Gambia, Kenya, Mauritania, Morocco, Zambia, Sudan, Tanganyika, Uganda, Upper Volta, Zanzibar.

activities through its remaining affiliates,[8] and has persisted in its policy concerning the approach to African unity.

THE AFRICAN TRADE UNION CONFEDERATION

The third organization, ATUC, formed in 1962 as a reaction against AATUF's stand on affiliation, crystallized the split in the trade union movement. It consisted originally of 21 ICFTU affiliates, 12 affiliates of the International Federation of Christian Trade Unions (IFCTU) and 8 independents. ATUC's original members were mostly unions from the countries which had formed the old Monrovia grouping, formally dissolved after the creation of the OAU. While the organization reflected to a great extent the philosophy of the ICFTU, it was, from the beginning, rent by internal problems. The ICFTU and the IFCTU were unable to agree on a major issue: namely, the number of trade union centers that were to exist at the national level. Also, ATUC had no full-time committed leadership: All of its officers held major positions in their national unions. Thus, it was essentially a paper organization with little evidence of overt activity.

After several postponements, ATUC held its Second Triennial Conference in Lagos, October 5-8, 1965. While the first conference in 1962 explicitly excluded the participation of delegates from international organizations, an ICFTU delegation was present and vocal at the 1965 conference, indicating that the position on affiliation stands firm despite considerable internal disagreement over the issue. Moreover, the new list of officers revealed few structural changes. Ten out of eighteen officers were in the same positions and other officers were mostly representative of the same countries as their predecessors. The roster was still dominated by Senegalese officers. Perpetuating the pragmatic orientation of ATUC, the conference focused upon steps to bridge economic inequalities as they affected the worker.

---

[8]During the period of waning influences the ICFTU International Solidarity Fund's general expenditures in Africa were as follows: 1961 - $699,454; 1962 - $987,618; 1963 - $735,083 (ICFTU, *op. cit.*, p. 309).

In view of the waning influence of the ICFTU, whose affiliates constitute the majority of ATUC's membership, the support of the organization is clearly precarious. However, that it exists as an internal African organization allows it the potentiality of someday absorbing the infrastructure of the external organizations, should their position on the continent become untenable.

* * *

It is clear from the character of the above developments that there are enormous difficulties blocking trade union unity. That the same issues recur at every conference is not fortuitous. There are several fundamental aspects of the African labor movement which lie at the root of these issues and which preclude a common organization at this time. First, the genuine need of unions for external assistance and its ready availability have led to the focus on the affiliation issue. Second, the role of labor as instrumental to realizing national political and economic goals increasingly orients the unions to the national level, obviating the significance of a centralized Pan-African organization.

THE AFFILIATION ISSUE

Once the split in the continental movement developed, there was only one brief period when some concurrence between the organizations seemed possible. Following the formation of the OAU in May, 1963, a surge of Pan-Africanism inspired a plan for an ATUC-AATUF merger. A joint committee was formed, but the plan broke down at an early stage of discussion over the perennial issues of international affiliation. Subsequent meetings of all three organizations have only made the differences between them more articulate.

THE NEED OF EXTERNAL SUPPORT

African trade unions are faced with great difficulty in trying to create financially and administratively autonomous organizations. Dues paying is erratic; while the members are willing to support union policies, they are often unwilling or unable to contribute regularly to union funds, a problem exacerbated by the inadequate procedures for dues handling. Although the check-off has been introduced in many countries and is, in many cases, compulsory, its implementation is often difficult and requires additional staff, which only adds to union expenses. Moreover, since the concept of voluntary activity is poorly developed, a large number of full-time leaders are required to keep the organizations functioning. The high expenditures for salaries as well as for offices, equipment, and administrative and organizational expenses have led unions to seek external financial support and, therefore, to have an external financial base.

Beyond these difficulties, unions are also faced with a chronic leadership shortage. Expanding rapidly in terms of constituency, unions are pressed for trained personnel. But the most highly trained personnel are usually attracted to the political movement, often regarding the unions as temporary channels of mobility. Faced with administrative disorganization, unions have been led increasingly to rely on the experience and training facilities offered from external sources. There is little indication that these dilemmas will disappear in the near future, considering the exigencies of rapid development. Moreover, the easy availability of aid of all types tends to discourage the development of internal self-sufficiency. Thus, to date, the unions are inextricably tied to support coming from sources outside their own organizations.

THE AVAILABILITY OF EXTERNAL SUPPORT

That the divisive issue of international affiliation has become so prominent in trade union affairs is due to the availability of a variety of sources of support which the unions cannot afford to turn away. Supported by international organizations, the continental groupings inevitably have become identified with one or another of the Cold War blocs. The ICFTU has openly encouraged this identification if only because it has pressed the right of unions to affiliate to international organizations. The WFTU adjusted more easily to an indirect approach, agreeing to AATUF's position on disaffiliation and, in a sense, gaining by doing so.

Affiliation with international organizations is imbued with many implications which are at variance with the essence of

Pan-Africanism. For Pan-Africanism has, in large part, embodied the xenophobia natural to newly independent nations. It was the experience of African unions during their formative period that external organizations represented ideological and political doctrines. This was particularly true in West Africa, where the unions were affiliated to a variety of politicized unions in France. It has, of course, more recently been reinforced by the attachments of the ICFTU and WFTU to Cold War alignments.[9]

These alignments are viewed with increasing suspicion by African political leaders. As early as January, 1957, when the ICFTU first convened in Accra to create a regional organization, some African leaders refused to attend because they felt that the ideological divisions of the world, as represented by the ICFTU, were contrary to African interests. Subsequently, spurred by the divisions that have occurred within their national labor movements, many political leaders have instituted a policy of non-affiliation to international organizations.

Thus, the ICFTU position in Africa has been considerably weakened and, as a result, the contributors to the ICFTU International Solidarity Fund have been increasingly dissatisfied with its operation. While most contributors have had some independent activity in Africa, most of their international activity has been channeled through the ICFTU. Recently, however, two of the main contributors to the International Solidarity Fund, the AFL-CIO and the German Trade Union Federation (DGB), have cut back their contribution by 25 per cent,[10] and have at the same time stepped up their independent programs on the continent.

An increasing variety of national organizations from both

---

[9] The WFTU, in 1958, had only 72,457 members in Africa, and 42 per cent of these were in the Union of South Africa, according to the U.S. Department of Labor, Office of International Labor Affairs, *Directory of the World Federation of Trade Unions* (Washington, D.C.: U.S. Government Printing Office, 1958). The extent of WFTU support of the continental organizations is impossible to ascertain. The ICFTU, through its general fund, expended $735,083 in 1964. Since 1962, this has been increasingly channeled through its regional machinery (ICFTU, *op. cit.*), pp. 304-9.
[10] *The New York Times*, March 15, 1965.

East and West, therefore, now offer financial aid, educational and technical service, equipment, etc. By and large, these national organizations have stayed out of the Pan-African sphere, focusing their efforts on national centers and on the training of leaders. A brief digression to describe some of their activities illustrates how these reinforce national institutions at the expense of Pan-Africanism.

THE HISTADRUT

The Histadrut program centers around the Afro-Asian Institute for Labor which was founded in 1960 with an annual budget of over $.5 million financed by Histadrut, plus scholarship contributions from the AFL-CIO. Its purpose is leadership training in social and economic as well as trade union matters. Histadrut has also had a significant influence on structural changes made in African unions following independence, notably in Ghana.[11]

AFRICAN-AMERICAN LABOR CENTER

The AFL-CIO has only recently begun to organize its activities in Africa through the African-American Labor Center (AALC) formed in January, 1965. The work of the AALC is largely to focus on social projects and problems related to economic development. Two existing AFL-CIO training centers in Nigeria and Kenya will be expanded, and a third, concentrating on trade and development, is projected. Asking for support by African unions "irrespective of their international affiliation,"[12] the AFL-CIO is obviously trying to move away from divisive issues of affiliation and free trade unionism. Rather, it has shifted to a less controversial area of development and social welfare which, however, is strictly a matter of national rather than continental concern. (The German, British, and other national trade union centers also have independent programs in Africa, offering scholarships, advice, and generally attempting to keep channels open to the West.)

---

[11] See Chapter Nine in Mordechai E. Kreinin, *Israel and Africa* (New York: Praeger, 1964).
[12] *African Labour News*, No. 150 (March 25, 1965).

EXTERNAL SUPPORT FROM THE EAST

National organizations from Eastern Europe offer competitive training programs and scholarships, send trade union advisors, and utilize similar means in seeking to develop influence in Africa.[13] The China Federation of Trade Unions has also been exchanging trade union delegations on an increasingly frequent basis, and moreover, has tried to exacerbate the Cold War aspects of the Pan-African organizations by supporting AATUF as a "vanguard" of the struggle against imperialism, and condemning ATUC as "sabotage by imperialism."[14]

THE INTERNATIONAL IMPACT ON PAN-AFRICANISM

Thus, there exists what has appropriately been described as an "international smorgasbord."[15] African trade unions can select from a complex array of competing programs, and these are all associated with Cold War alignments. The effects of these programs on labor's predilection to Pan-Africanism can be summarized as follows:

(1) By bringing divisive Cold War issues into the trade union movement, two factions are established. All relationships tend to be interpreted as either Communist, on the one hand, or neocolonialist on the other, and the Pan-African trade union organizations have become immediately polarized in this way.

(2) While those supporting the unions are often vocal in backing Pan-Africanism, money has gone by and large to na-

---

[13] While a systematic survey of these activities is not feasible with available resources, it is known that there are trade union training schools and centers with a significant African enrollment in Budapest (organized in 1959), Leipzig (1960), Prague (1960) and in Tashkent (1961). Both the WFTU and the East German FDGB have also contributed to establishing training centers within Africa.

[14] United States Consulate, *Survey of China Mainland Press*, No. 2512 (June 2, 1961), p. 64; and No. 2672 (January 28, 1962), p.24.

[15] Fred G. Burke, *Africa's Quest for Order* (Englewood Cliffs: Prentice-Hall, 1964), p. 124.

tional centers and to the training of leaders who will use their education at the national level. This is increasingly true as the European and American unions have furthered their independent activities in Africa. As their support increasingly focuses on economic and social development, it serves further to reinforce national orientations. While this is not necessarily antithetical to Pan-Africanism, it does little to draw interest in the continental direction.

(3) The choice that unions have in availing themselves of assistance has resulted in divisions and conflicts within national unions. These have led to political takeover of unions to preserve national stability. This is clearly the case in the events in Kenya in 1965. In June, the Minister of Labor announced that the factions in the labor movement had caused a significant increase in strikes. Shortly thereafter, the government dissolved the competing groups and established COTU. With increasing control of this sort, unions are precluded from acting independently in contributing to African unity at the trade union level.

THE NATIONAL ORIENTATION OF LABOR

The national orientation of African trade unions is not unusual: It is characteristic that trade unions everywhere tend to focus on a level where they can effectively operate. In fact, there are many interesting parallels that can be drawn between the reaction, on the one hand, of European trade unions to European economic integration and, on the other, of the Africans to Pan-Africanism.

Despite the high prosperity in Europe and the relatively equitable wage level between various European nations, many unions were opposed to integration. In the Scandinavian countries belonging to the European Free Trade Area, where unions were closely associated with the government, unions were reluctant to jeopardize their recent social and economic gains by allowing national policies to be controlled by intergovernmental organizations. Trade unions in Switzerland opposed joining the Common Market in order to preserve the benefits of lower tariff barriers. And a group in the British Trades

Union Congress, reflecting the suspicions of the British worker and his fear that European labor would undermine his wages, opposed the idea of free movement of labor that was implied by integration. The split on this issue within the TUC certainly added to the reluctance of the Labor Party to support the European Economic Community (EEC).[16]

Similarly, in Africa, it is not only external pressures which have led unions to focus on the national level but internal circumstances as well; and these assumed an even more salient role than in Europe, considering the wage differential between nations and the exigencies of rapid development. These circumstances can be analyzed in terms of three factors: the role of unions in national economic development, their political orientation, and the diversity in the power of unions in different nations. These three factors will be developed here only briefly as they relate to the problems of Pan-Africanism.

ROLE OF UNIONS IN NATIONAL DEVELOPMENT

Envisioning unions as instruments of national development, national governments are increasingly imposing legislative controls on union activities. At the same time, they are trying to build them into viable organizations that will effectively implement their economic plans. The extent of legislative action restricting trade unions has ranged from a state of total takeover in Ghana and Tanganyika to the relatively autonomous situation that exists in Nigeria. But everywhere the tendency is toward greater government restriction justified by the economic needs of the nation.[17] Their role

---

[16]For further discussion of issues relating to trade unions and European integration, see R. C. Beever, "Trade Unions and the Common Market," *Planning* (Political and Economic Planning), Vol. XXVIII (May 1, 1962), pp. 73-109. Also, B. Seidman, "Trade Union Views on European Economic Integration," *Monthly Labor Review*, Vol. LXXXIII, No. 4 (April, 1960), pp. 365-69.

[17]Even in Nigeria there have been appeals for legislative controls over international affiliation and the financial affairs of unions. See, for example, *West Africa* (March 24, 1962), p. 2388; and (September 1, 1962), p. 969. More recently, grumblings deploring strike activity indicate that the Federal Government has been considering means of strike control; cf. *West Africa* (September 11, 1965), p. 1026.

as productionist organizations delineated, the unions are increasingly focusing on the national level, having no pragmatic basis for extending activities beyond it. In any case, national governments apparently are extremely reluctant to allow unions to extend their activities beyond the range of national control.

The difficulties encountered in developing a common policy on labor problems in the East African Common Services Organization is a good case in point. East African trade union leaders have repeatedly acknowledged their support of East African Federation and the formation of an East African trade union. Meeting in Nairobi in August, 1963, to discuss the coordination of trade union activities, for example, the East African union leaders resolved to form a trade union federation to support political federation. Yet, nothing was to come of this. For recognizing the implications of federal citizenship in federation, the political leaders saw that federation could exacerbate rather than resolve the labor problem.

One of the arguments used against establishing federal citizenship, in fact, was the problem of free mobility of labor. Kenya, because of her early development of industrial centers, had a reservoir of semiskilled labor which has migrated to other territories. Kenyan workers, for example, constitute about 10 per cent of the labor force in Uganda. Uganda, on the other hand, while dependent upon Kenyan labor, needs to maintain some control over labor mobility in order to resolve her own problems of unemployment. Legislation subsequently has been enacted to restrict participation of non-Ugandans in the trade unions, and Ugandan negotiators have generally resisted federation, using labor as an obstructing issue:

> Uganda wanted to restrict the movement of labor which would not be possible with common citizenship... If people could come to Uganda as they liked then the country's efforts to raise standards would be in vain.

---

[18] A Statement by Adoko A. Nekyon, Minister for Planning and Development, explaining his position in a National Assembly debate. This, and the above case, are discussed in greater detail in Roger Scott, "Labor Legislation and the Federation Issue," *East Africa Journal* (November, 1964).

While this example pertains to the particular problem of labor migration, the exigencies of national development are such that wage policies, Africanization policies and other issues related to labor are similarly tied to the national arena.

POLITICAL ORIENTATION OF LABOR

That African unions rely to a great extent upon social legislation enacted by national governments in order to satisfy many of the demands that they would ordinarily win through union negotiations is a further impediment to Pan-Africanism. While particularly true of the ex-French territories which followed traditional practices established in France, the government everywhere plays a protective role for the unions and for labor. Employing a large percentage of the employed labor force as the largest single employer by far in each country, African governments further reinforce this relationship. Also, governments have historically set the wage patterns for the national economy.

In consequence, the economic issues of concern to unions quite logically often become translated into political issues which are essentially national, since the unions' economic success and their ultimate power is essentially cast in this national framework. In turn, labor's focus on national concerns tends to distract the labor movements from forming a continental organization which, in any case, could offer the unions little in the way of concrete political or economic advantages that they could not win at home.

Problems of leadership that plague all the continental organizations are another manifestation of this focus on the national rather than the continental scene. For while the national trade union centers are a steppingstone to political power at the national level, the continental organizations tend to lead nowhere politically. Thus, with few exceptions, the officials of all the continental organizations remain committed to their national trade union centers.

DIVERSITY IN UNION POWER

Standing in the way of political Pan-Africanism, very

practical problems have also blocked agreement in the Pan-African labor field. The considerable differences in economic and industrial development with a concomitant disparity in the size of the labor force have posed serious problems. Combined with the inherent differences from dissimilar colonial experiences, the wide diversity among African trade unions practically precludes the uniformity in policy that Pan-Africanism implies.

On the one hand, those unions which are intrinsically the strongest are unwilling to give up anything for the sake of Pan-African organization. On the other, the weaker unions are concerned that they will be overwhelmed by the stronger. Thus, Ghana's predominant role in AATUF has been suspect. John Tettegah, for example, was denied entry into Nigeria in July, 1964, on the grounds that he was a "confusionist," who was contributing to the split in the Nigerian trade union movement.[19] Indeed, power politics has been an important hindrance to the formation of a united Pan-African organization, but is particularly apparent in AATUF.

While it remains a moot point whether regional groupings are in fact Pan-African movements or, rather, represent merely tendencies toward "Balkanization," the dichotomy between the ideals of unity and the hard realities that any movement for regional federation faces is obviously as serious at the truly Pan-African level. As for the hard realities that any labor movement must face regarding national sovereignty in mere regional federation, these are apparent in some of the issues obstructing East African federation.

A Marco Surveys poll taken in all three East African territories in early 1964 when federation became a public issue, for example, revealed that an overwhelming majority were in favor of federation. Of those interviewed, 96.5 per cent in Kenya, 88 per cent in Uganda and 82.5 per cent in Tanganyika desired East African unity.[20] Yet practical matters related to national interests precluded its success. Thus, stringent labor laws enacted in Tanganyika in 1962 evoked a defensive reaction among the other East African states. Speaking for Uganda at

---

[19]*African Labour News*, No. 121 (July 29, 1964).
[20]*Tanganyika Standard*, April 1, 1964.

LABOR: STUMBLING BLOCK TO PAN-AFRICANISM   137

the Working Party's meeting on East African federation held in Kampala in May 1964, Adoko Nekyon took issue with the Tanganyikan regulations: He did not wish them to be imposed on the rest of East Africa. Also, the Working Party was split on the matter of trade unions: Uganda took the position that unions should be a matter of state concern, while Kenya countered that this was impractical in view of the interterritorial functions of the East African Common Services Organization.[21]

National rather than regional interests in labor matters also prevailed at a conference on federation held at the University of East Africa in November 1963. While claiming that there was no need of formal integration of labor with the proposed government of an East African federation, Tom Mboya stated in his speech that "labor policy should be within the competence of a federal government rather than remaining under national jurisdiction." But he thereby provoked some searching questions which dealt with issues such as the movement of labor across national boundaries, the discrepancies in the levels of employment, and the probable dominance of Tanganyikan labor policy "because the least liberal usually prevails."[22] The questions clearly reveal, of course, that labor problems remain nationally oriented in terms of both the needs of national development and political control.

CONCLUSION

While still ideologically attractive, Pan-Africanism has been gradually losing ground to the national interests of the African labor movements, if merely out of practical considerations. One step further removed, international affiliations naturally also suffer as African unions focus more and more on their national interests. Apparently riding the wave of the increasing paramountcy of African national interests, AATUF has gained increasing support in African labor unions at the expense of the internationals. But that national interests are also increasing at the expense of continental considerations

---

[21] *Tanganyika Standard*, June 2, 1964.
[22] *Tanganyika Standard*, November 30, 1963.

ironically also spells sure opposition to AATUF. Liberian President William Tubman's description of union government as "Kwame's hobby" is indicative of the feeling of many Africans in this regard,[23] since Ghana's overwhelming predominance in AATUF has posed a threat to the national interests of the other African labor unions. Moreover, AATUF's bias towards centrality and uniformity, so disparate with the existing diversity and nationalist orientation, attenuates its Pan-African potentiality.

Finally, the inescapable flavor of foreign influence that permeates the unions at both the national and continental level is totally at odds with Pan-Africanism, which seeks to avoid foreign commitments, as the following OAU resolution testifies:[24]

> Convinced that national rivalries, international disputes and bloc politics alien to this continent and its problems threaten almost daily intrusion into African life... (the Assembly resolves that) member states should avoid all commitments, alliances, undertakings and agreements which tend to inject into Africa foreign rivalries or bloc powers, or which would tend directly or indirectly to create tensions, conflicts or disputes in Africa between African states.

Trade unions are, at this time, extremely vulnerable to foreign rivalries. The continental groupings merely reflect this vulnerability, since they originate and are sustained almost entirely from external sources. Their crucial weakness lies in this very fact: Developed on a base other than that of the national trade union centers, they cannot be representative of African trade union objectives. The erratic development of continental union organization illustrates the distance separating Pan-Africanism in its ideological manifestation from its organizational reality.

---

[23]President Tubman made the statement following the OAU Conference held in Accra in October, 1965. *The New York Times*, October 27, 1965.

[24]"Resolution of the first Assembly of the Heads of State and Government of the OAU," Cairo, July, 1964, in Legum, *op. cit.*, Appendix 26.

CHAPTER **8** AFRICAN TRADE UNIONS AND THE COLD WAR

George E. Lichtblau[†]

The purpose of this chapter is not to give a detailed history of rival international trade unions in postwar Africa, but to describe the framework in which they operate. The political behavior of African trade unions is analyzed within the context of the so-called Cold War by focusing mainly on two sets of complementary considerations:

1. How international trade union politics follow the patterns of international relations among governments and how these relations with Africa and in Africa have changed, both on the national and trade union levels, with the changing character of the Cold War;

2. How the African trade unions use their international ties in their domestic alliance policies and how these uses relate to the political expectations of their foreign allies.

[†]George E. Lichtblau holds the position of Specialist, International Labor Affairs, in the U.S. Department of State. The author of numerous articles on trade unions in the developing areas, Mr. Lichtblau has also lectured on the subject in various universities. He toured Europe and Africa in 1964-65 as a Rockefeller Research Fellow. The views and opinions he expresses in this chapter are his own and should in no way be interpreted as reflecting the official policy of either the U.S. Government or the U.S. Department of State.

STATES AND UNIONS IN ALLIANCE

It has become almost axiomatic that loyalties to either domestic or foreign power interests are the chief motivating forces of trade unions for their involvement in international affairs; for this reason, it is not unrealistic to speak of trade union diplomacy. Formal declarations of mutual support, intervention on behalf of allies with international authorities, national governments, and employers, as well as a system of technical and financial assistance, reinforce the parallel with governmental diplomacy. The commitment to governmental power interests holds more true of the aid-giving international and national trade union organizations but--as I shall discuss later--requires that some allowance be made for the political and trade union changes taking place on the African scene. In cases of competing movements or competing factions within movements, each looking for rival international support, or where relations between unions and their governments remain as yet vaguely defined, it would be difficult to argue that the aid recipients and aid donors would necessarily have strong common national or international political or ideological identities.

Trade union diplomacy as an element of international power politics is a relatively new phenomenon and constitutes a radical departure from the trade union internationalism existing before World War II, which to some extent survived on the non-Communist side as an important factor in the establishment of the World Federation of Trade Unions (WFTU) in 1945. This internationalism was based on the solidarity of protest against social and economic injustices, both in national and international affairs, which had been epitomized by Fascism and Nazism. The Soviet Union sought to exploit this protest aspect of the WFTU to its own advantage. But the character of the labor and socialist movements in the West changed in the postwar world, when they attained ready access to governments and when the main enemies were no longer a revived Fascism or a ruthless social order exploiting the workers, but the "socialist bloc" which had come into existence under the aegis of the Red Army.

When the Western democratic trade unions became part of the establishment, not only did they shed all vestiges of revolutionary intent and Marxist ideology, but any threat to the establishment became also a threat to themselves. The old ambivalence of the Socialists toward the Communists virtually disappeared, and hence "free labor" confronted the bloc trade unions and their allies, just as the Western governments confronted the bloc governments. When, after the Korean armistice and Stalin's death, the Cold War shifted from a power deadlock in Europe and insurrection in Asian and Pacific areas (reoccupied by the Western powers from the Japanese) to primarily diplomatic contests for the alignment of the countries emerging from colonial rule, the trade union internationals and their key affiliates correspondingly changed their focus of interest and their tactics. They even shifted their regional interests as international attention shifted from crises in Asia to new crisis centers in the Middle East and Africa. And with these reductions in Cold War tensions, both governmental and international trade union diplomacy veered increasingly from a polarized power and ideological East-West axis to regional and bilateral relations.

Generally, the big internationals--i.e., the World Federation of Trade Unions (WFTU) and the International Confederation of Free Trade Unions (ICFTU), and their leading members, such as the Soviet All Union Central Council of Trade Unions (AUCCTU) and the AFL-CIO--prefer ideological commitments. Both displayed this tendency at the 1965 congresses of their respective internationals. Thus, in order to counter the centrifugal trends within these movements, U.S. labor pleaded for strengthening the anti-Communist orientation of the ICFTU, and the Soviets sought to evoke before the WFTU an image of the Western powers as a menace in propaganda terms reminiscent of the Stalin era. In the end both yielded to the impracticality of making their respective points stick. While most other affiliated or allied unions also continue to defer to the principles for which their respective internationals stand, they do so with varying reservations where ideology interferes with their own national or trade union considerations, such as trade or foreign relations.

Even the leading members of the two internationals display considerable flexibility in the application of their avowed principles for the sake of overriding policy considerations, but interpret any form of cooperation, from formal alignment to informal multilateral or bilateral arrangements, as a test of ideological commitment. Moreover, with surprising similarity in this respect, they have not hesitated to belittle and downgrade their internationals along with the concessions they have had to make to the divergent interests and tendencies among their lesser allies. However, the display of disunity and ideological deviation is much more dramatic in the WFTU, in which the Soviets play a guiding role which the American labor movement has never had in the ICFTU. As a result of this autonomist trend we have on the Western side the AFL-CIO, the West German Trade Union Federation (DGB), the Israeli Histadrut, the Belgian General Federation of Labor (FGTB), the Austrian Trade Union Federation (OGB), and others operating independently outside the framework of the ICFTU, to which they all belong. And, of course, the separate activities of the Chinese Communists are taken for granted.

In contrast to the big aid-giving unions, the aid-receiving unions from the nonaligned countries in Africa prefer international relations to be explicitly tactical, requiring only a minimum of ideological commitment, while permitting a maximum of benefits and political flexibility. An increasing number of African unions have abandoned their formal affiliations--although more often at the behest of their governments and ruling parties than of their own volition--substituting instead less formal relations, some involving little more than accepting money or technical assistance. Whatever their ideological sympathies, the Africans did not wish their causes used for the promotion of the larger causes of others, but wanted mainly to enlist international movements in the service of their own causes. In the long run, however, the divergent trends of Africans becoming increasingly preoccupied with finding a new ideology for themselves while the rest of the world moves away from ideology, their insistence on the reversal of established power relations between the weak and the strong, and their unwillingness to define their relations with the outside world in any but *ad hoc* terms, pose a danger of growing isolation of Africa from the mainstream of world politics.[1] Disillusionment has already affected aid programs and trade union relations in both the Western and Soviet camps. On the political level, it is even spreading to the nonaligned nations of Asia and Latin America. Moreover, in the labor field it has produced a side effect: Western assist-

---

[1]See Aimé Césaire, "lettre à Maurice Thorez," *Présence Africaine* (Paris, 1956), p. 12: "What I want is that Marxism and Communism be placed in the service of the black peoples and not the black peoples in the service of Marxism and Communism."

ance has been financed increasingly by governments and managed and distributed by special foundations in which the trade unions act merely as sponsors.

THE INTERNATIONALS AND THE INDEPENDENCE STRUGGLE

The internationals focused their attention on the development of the African trade unions as primarily political protest movements. As long as labor protests were directed against colonialism, sympathetic foreign labor movements could bring to bear international pressures and agitation which made the colonial authorities increasingly reluctant to curb the unions' freedom to demonstrate their grievances, to organize, to strike, or to bargain. In return for their ability to protect the unions in the newly emerging African countries, the internationals expected the continuation of their influence after independence to assure the perpetuation of common ideological and political principles. However, as the African tolerance for protest--especially protest supported from the outside--diminished after independence, so did the roles of the internationals. The new African authorities saw little distinction between support of rights and encouragement of opposition. Even an implicit defense arrangement with outsiders evoked anxieties among the African leaders, the more so if it came from the suspect West, which seemed to them to be seizing any pretext to demonstrate African ineptness in governing. Perversely, many African governments developed greater tolerance for the more radical internationals, such as the WFTU and the All African Trade Union Federation (AATUF), because they tended to externalize trade union protest, directing it against international rather than local grievances, and endorsed governmental control in the name of "socialism." This, of course, was a trend not readily apparent when the ICFTU entered the African scene.

During the transition to independence of most African countries, the different views of international trade union ties of aid donors and aid recipients remained relatively unimportant. The main problem of decolonization had to be settled within the political systems of the colonial powers and the Western alliance. While ideological identification with Marxism-Leninism and its equation of anti-imperialism with the universal class struggle provided considerable satisfaction for many African nationalists, open or covert ties with the Soviet camp offered little leverage in the struggle for independence in Africa. Nor were the Soviets or the WFTU initially prepared to give substantial financial or other trade union assistance to the Africans. In Africa under colonial rule, the WFTU or the Soviet bloc unions had very little direct access to newly emerging unions. Thus the ICFTU became easily the most important and the most attractive international trade union movement. Moreover, the ICFTU's avowed anti-Communism was predicated on the larger issue of democratic freedom and self-determination, which included full support of the independence aspirations and socio-economic grievances of the colonial trade unions.

THE INTERNATIONALS IN THE BRITISH COLONIES

During the preindependence period, most unions in the English-speaking areas followed the guidance of the British Trades Union Congress (TUC) and joined the WFTU; broke with it when it split in January, 1949; and subsequently aligned with the ICFTU. Although only three African unions (from Sierra Leone, Gambia, and Mauritius) participated in the founding congress of the ICFTU in London in December, 1949, as the number of African unions increased, they joined the Free International, persuaded by their British trade union contacts and/or the trade union advisers and other officials of the colonial Labor Departments. Thus trade union federations from nearly all English-speaking African territories belonged at some time to the ICFTU.

As long as the British retained responsibility in African territories, the TUC assumed a protective role over the trade unions, watched over labor legislation and labor policy, served as an intermediary in strikes and times of crisis, and maintained regular contacts through correspondence, invitations, visits by British trade union leaders and advisers, educational assistance, and occasional contributions of money and equipment. But the TUC gradually shifted its role of assistance to the ICFTU and the International Trade Secretariats

(ITS),[2] in whose African operations British personnel continued to play an important role.

To the extent that African trade union leaders and movements in the British territories sought contacts with Communist and militant leftist groups, they did so largely with the British Communist Party; Communist-led unions, such as the Electrical Trades' Union or the National Union of Mineworkers; or the Trades' Union Committee of the Movement for Colonial Freedom (MCF). The MCF, especially, served as a useful United Front consisting of Communists, left-wing as well as more orthodox Labor Party MP's, and members of professional, academic, and student groups opposed to colonialism. The only two WFTU affiliates in English-speaking Africa were the Sudan Workers' Trades Union Federation and the South African Trade Union Council, both of which were aligned with local Communist parties. Both also maintained ties with the British labor movement, in which Communist and fellow-traveling elements were far from isolated, despite the anti-Communism of the TUC General Secretary and the Chairman of its International Department. In a few other instances, such as Ghana and Nigeria during the early 1950's, militant trade union elements identified themselves with the WFTU in their challenge to the ascendancy of the leading nationalist parties and their allied unions, which threatened to exclude them. In both cases the leaders obtained some financial and moral support from the bloc, but their unions did not formally affiliate with the WFTU. Although their challenge was ideological and tactical over the shaping of the independence struggle, underlying it were tribal, regional, and personal rivalries.

Whereas the links with the left-wing groups were ideologically and psychologically more satisfying to the African and other colonial labor leaders, they readily appreciated that, in matters of practical politics, contacts with the TUC, the Fabian Colonial Bureau, and the Labor Party, in or out of power, were more useful. These organizations provided more authoritative spokesmen on colonial issues in Parliament and had more ready access to officials in the Colonial Office and the colonial governments and to overseas employers. And, above all, the

---

[2]The International Trade Secretariats are functional international federations operating in specific or related trades or industries throughout the world in close cooperation with the ICFTU.

TUC could provide considerable protection and prestige to a growing number of African labor leaders who not only received training under British trade union auspices but also acquired their first practical experience in politics through their involvement with the various segments of the British labor movement (which includes the trade unions, the Labor Party, and other groups of various socialist hues).

The subsequent affiliation of the African unions with the ICFTU extended this alliance system with the British labor movement to the U.S. labor movement with its greater financial resources, its linkage to the U.S. political scene, its militant anticolonialism, and its freedom from concern with the political or trade union consequences of encouraging nationalist independence movements. It dramatically changed the nature and the horizon of the African trade union alliances with the outside world. These indirect involvements of the African labor and political leaders with British and American political pressure and interest groups through their international trade union ties reinforced their natural penchant for extraparliamentary and protest politics. In this respect the appeal of alliances with ICFTU, the British and American labor movements, and other Western trade unions was not unlike that of the Communist movement, with its conspiratorial tactics and alliances offered to those who either are excluded or exclude themselves from their political systems.

Initially, ICFTU activities in the British colonial countries remained largely under TUC influence, providing additional training facilities, enlarging contacts with both African and non-African trade union leaders, and giving guidance, support, and publicity for economic, social and political grievances. Like the International Labor Organization (ILO), the ICFTU enhanced the TUC's own leverage with its government in influencing labor and social policies in the colonies. This role of the ICFTU as an outside pressure group greatly increased in the wake of the 1956-57 Suez crisis, when the American labor movement insisted on assuming a leading role, both on its own account and in ICFTU activities in sub-Saharan Africa. Thereafter TUC influence in the ICFTU decreased.

At the first African Regional Conference of the ICFTU, held in Accra in January, 1957, the Americans and the British clashed openly over supporting the political aspirations of the

African trade unions, over the degree of intervention in colonial labor affairs, and over TUC reluctance to take a more aggressive anticolonial stand. The U.S. trade union spokesmen compared British and French colonialism with Communist oppression behind the Iron Curtain and aligned themselves with the nationalist sentiments of the Africans. Moreover, for the first time, the AFL-CIO promised substantial financial assistance in the building of trade union headquarters, especially in Ghana and Kenya, through its William Green Memorial Fund. It also offered, through ICFTU affiliation, new channels of communication with the State Department; members of Congress who were willing to support African causes; the liberal and academic community, which was just becoming aware of Africa; and the politically awakening American Negro community. The AFL-CIO thus reinforced U.S. pressures toward rapid decolonization of Africa by making the ICFTU available to aspiring trade union and nationalist leaders as a new forum and instrument for dramatizing African causes in the U.S., in the UN, and the ILO. Alignment with the ICFTU further served as a reassuring gesture that the Africans, by availing themselves of its services, were rejecting the anti-imperialist campaign of the Soviet camp. British sensitivity to this campaign showed its effectiveness.

THE INTERNATIONALS IN THE FRENCH COLONIES

In the French-speaking areas, international trade union ties played a significant role only in the independence struggles of the North African countries. Here the role of the U.S. labor movement in defiance of French public and trade union attitudes contributed to the decolonizing pressures and prevented the rise of serious trade union conflicts over international alignment during the independence struggle. Instead the Communist segments of the labor movement submerged in the nationalist unions. Both Tunisia and Morocco enjoyed internal autonomy, and neither their political institutions nor their trade unions were as closely interwoven with the French parties and unions as those of other French African territories. Thus the Tunisian General Federation of Labor (UGTT) and the Moroccan Labor Federation (UMT) detached themselves from the French General Confederation of Labor (CGT) even before their respective independence struggles and established their own outside ties.[3] Both chose the ICFTU and the AFL-CIO as their main allies, and through them gained U.S. support and sympathy against French colonial intransigence.

As the rebellion which had started in November, 1954, mounted in Algeria, both Tunisia and Morocco gave sanctuary to the National Liberation Front (FLN), and their trade unions assisted the Federation of Algerian Workers (UGTA), which was organized in February, 1956.[4] Under their influence the UGTA affiliated with the ICFTU, and through it sought American and other Western trade union and governmental support for the FLN (with which it was aligned), as well as assistance for its own exile operations, especially in the field of training. (It is significant that the ICFTU, conscious of its primary diplomatic role, accepted the UGTA despite its ideological affinity to revolutionary Marxism, rather than its more moderate rival, the United Trade Union Federation of Algerian Workers (USTA),[5] whose membership was primarily drawn from the Algerian workers in France and which lacked the confidence of the FLN leadership.) The UGTA also established informal relations with the WFTU through an International Trade Union Committee for Solidarity with the Algerian Workers and People, and obtained political and financial support as well as cadre and vocational training from bloc trade unions. But while accepting Communists within its ranks and cadres, it restricted their role and influence, thus satisfying the requirements of the ICFTU.

Although all three North African trade union federations had made formal commitments only to the ICFTU during their formative stages and their independence struggles, once the entire Maghreb was free of French rule the utility of these ties diminished, especially since American assistance and influence did not supplant French interests and aid. Both the UMT and

---

[3] *Union Générale Tunisienne du Travail (UGTT), Union Marocaine du Travail (UMT), Confédération Générale du Travail (CFT).*
[4] *Front de Libération Nationale (FLN), Union Générale des Travailleurs Algériens (UGTA).*
[5] *Union des Syndicats des Travailleurs Algériens (USTA).*

the UGTA withdrew their affiliation in 1963.[6]

Even before that, they had affiliated with the All African Trade Union Federation (AATUF), established contacts with the United Arab Republic-controlled International Confederation of Arab Trade Unions (ICATU), and sought to assume pivotal roles in alliances between the Afro-Asian unions, the Yugoslavs and the WFTU in common opposition to the continuation of ICFTU activities in the emerging nations. Hence, for domestic and foreign policy reasons, demonstrations of their "anti-imperialist-socialist" orientation overshadowed the need for assistance or ties with the Western unions. But because of cultural and ideological affinities, the UMT and the UGTA continue to maintain contacts with the French unions, especially the CGT and the Christian CFTC.[7] Other Western trade union presence in both countries was reduced to a small German training program in Morocco and some German and U.S. trade union assistance in Algeria given outside the ICFTU in the hope of keeping the door to the West open.

Only the Tunisian UGTT retains its ties with the ICFTU as acknowledgment of the importance of American support and

---

[6] The UGTA announced its withdrawal in July 1963, following strong ICFTU protests against government purges of the top Algerian labor leaders over the issues of subordination to the FLN at the First National UGTA Congress in January, 1963, in the presence of a large ICFTU delegation. The UMT stopped paying its affiliation. It took the final decision to disaffiliate in April, 1963. While valid in general terms, the statement that the Maghreb labor movements made formal commitments only to the ICFTU should be qualified. For the UGTT affiliated first with the WFTU in 1949 and did not formally break these ties, in fact, until 1951, when it affiliated with the ICFTU. Also, although the diminishing importance of American assistance and influence was a major factor in the UMT and UGTA withdrawal of affiliation with the ICFTU, a resurgence of French interests and aid, implicitly vis-à-vis these two Maghreb labor movements, was negligible, if not absent altogether, in their decision to disaffiliate, particularly in the case of the UMT. Instead, radical Pan-Africanism was a paramount factor. See Willard A. Beling, *Modernization and African Labor: A Tunisian Case Study* (New York: Praeger, 1965).

[7] Now *Confédération Française Démocratique du Travail (CFDT)*. In Africa, the Christian unions substituted *Croyant* or "believing" for "Christian," since they also included Moslem and other non-Christian members.

aid, both on the governmental and trade union levels. But here, too, the commitment is on a much reduced scale, and the government's removal of some long-standing friends of some ICFTU and AFL-CIO leaders from the UGTT executive has strained relations, especially with the Americans. This disregard of ICFTU and U.S. sensitivities, accompanied by the diminishing interest of the Tunisian labor leadership in international as well as African affairs, is yet another sign that old international trade union ties have lost much of their significance.

To a large extent, the role which the ICFTU began to play in Tunisia in 1951,[8] and then continued in Morocco and Algeria, influenced the pattern of its operations in the rest of Africa. Similarly, the fearful cost of French intransigence to decolonization in North Africa influenced British policy in its African colonies. Consequently, despite the many misgivings of the British TUC and British colonial authorities over AFL-CIO and American-directed ICFTU activities in the process of orderly decolonization, they developed considerable tolerance for these intermediary links with the nationalist movements. Moreover, the shared belief in the ultimate right of the colonial people to independence and the TUC's support of the Americans in North Africa prevented the British labor movement from protesting too vigorously against later American pressures and activities in British territories. In this it differed greatly from the socialist Confédération Générale du Travail-Force Ouvrière (CGT-FO), which despite its membership in the ICFTU, opposed ICFTU activities as acts of Anglo-American imperialism until independence had been established. But, of course, with its African branches, the CGT-FO was far more directly affected by the independence movement in the colonies than the TUC.

Elsewhere in French-speaking Africa, both the WFTU and the ICFTU were virtually excluded from a direct role prior to the achievement of independence; this despite the fact that the French affiliates of the two internationals had branches in all the colonies and that one West African, Abdullaye Diallo, became a Vice-President of the WFTU. In the main, they were

---

[8]For an account of the early international relations of the UGTT, see Willard A. Beling, "WFTU and Decolonization: A Tunisian Case Study," *Journal of Modern African Studies*, Vol. II, No. 4 (1964), pp. 551-64.

barred from direct contacts in the colonies by the French authorities. However, their lack of access was also due to the opposition of the French unions themselves to intervention with their overseas branches by outsiders or to foreign encouragement of nationalist orientation of the newly emerging autonomous unions. Thus in French Africa, just as in the British areas, the first important outside political contacts were with the parties of the Left in Paris, especially with the Communists (PCF), the Socialists (SFIO), and the Christian Democrats (MRP), as well as with their trade union branches.[9]

Again, initially these contacts were mainly to engender extraparliamentary pressure through alliances with French parties and individual deputies willing to act as spokesmen for African interests and to persuade the parties to give more emphasis to these interests in their programs. But in the postwar period the French, unlike the British, sought far greater institutional integration of their colonies with the metropole. Not only did the colonial trade unions develop as part of the French labor movement, but the African parties themselves emerged originally with the aid of the PCF and the SFIO. African attachment to these parties stemmed from the Popular Front period and their support in 1946 of constitutional changes which would have provided immediate internal self-government and parliamentary institutions for each territory of a French federation. These ties remained important in the training and assistance of the first African representatives sent to the French Assembly in 1946. But soon African interests in these alliances diminished, with the exclusion of the Communists from the government in 1947, governmental pressures to discourage such alliances, the patently nationalist orientation of the French Communists and Socialists who denied special status to African nationalism in the name of "socialist internationalism," and subsequent French Government concessions to the political aspirations of the Africans in order to maintain the loyalties of the African dependencies. After the Bloc Démocratique Sénégalais (BDS) detached itself from the SFIO and the Rassemblement Démocratique Africain (RDA) broke with the Communists, the trend toward Africanization and autonomy spread to the trade unions.

In the end, de Gaulle's concession to the Black African

---

[9]*Parti Communiste Française* (PCF), *Section Française de l'Internationale Ouvrière* (SFIO), *Mouvement de Rassemblement Populaire* (MRP).

territories and their subsequent independence resulted more from his efforts to settle the Algerian conflict than from political pressures exerted by the African nationalists themselves through their political allies. Hence the Africans had little need to engage outside political and trade union pressures on their behalf for inducing policy changes by the French, or alternately, for supporting resistance movements. Moreover, despite its many grievances against colonial rule, the political and trade union elite remained too French-oriented to think of political solutions in which alliances outside the French sphere would have proved useful. Thus, prior to independence, neither the WFTU nor the ICFTU played a significant role in these territories beyond providing a few contacts and occasional training opportunities abroad.

This restriction of African political interests to the French political sphere, however, ended with the growing autonomy in French Black Africa after the passage of the *Louis Cadre* in 1956. On the trade union scene, the extension of outside contacts accompanied the efforts of Sekou Touré of Guinea to detach the West African trade unions from their French ties and to unite them in a regional federation, which he proposed as the center of a new Pan-African movement. Touré started this campaign at a meeting of the RDA Coordinating Committee in Conakry in 1955, with a plea for establishing an autonomous regional labor movement which was to parallel a strong political federation of the territories of French West Africa for dealing jointly with France.

After Touré had been expelled from the CGT for his declaration at the Conakry RDA meeting, about half of the CGT unions followed him into his new Confédération Générale des Travailleurs d'Afrique (CGTA). Subsequently, under WFTU and French CGT and Communist pressure, the West African CGT union joined with Touré's CGTA to form the Union Générale des Travailleurs d'Afrique Noire (UGTAN) in Cotonou in January, 1957. Touré assumed firm control of the movement, gave the CGT leader Abdoulaye Diallo only a secondary role, and in 1959, removed him from the trade union scene to a diplomatic post. UGTAN declared itself nonaligned but willing to enter fraternal relations with all internationals. Indeed, it contacted the ICFTU, the WFTU, the CGT and the AFL-CIO, and took advantage of the new confidence among the nonaligned forces in the post-Suez atmosphere to call for the formation of a Pan-African movement.

The new movement proved highly successful in rallying the unions of West Africa, even though the Christian and the rather small CGT-FO unions remained outside. In the referendum campaign of 1958, UGTAN, together with the RDA youth groups and students, became a major force opposing continued association with France, thus breaking the unity of the RDA, most of whose leaders favored an affirmative vote. When Guinea alone opted to leave the French community, UGTAN became increasingly suspect as a channel for Guinean-inspired, pro-bloc subversive activities. This suspicion was reinforced when the January, 1959, UGTAN Congress at Conakry declared itself a Pan-African movement, accepted the Ghana TUC as the first affiliate from a non-French territory, and openly avowed its sympathies with the WFTU and the "anti-imperialist camp." But soon the movement became a mere façade outside Guinea, and the majority of UGTAN sections began to disappear. Either they were dissolved by the suspicious governments of the new French West African successor states and then reconstituted themselves into their original components, as in Senegal, Ivory Coast, Dahomey, and Niger, or they disaffiliated *en bloc* and set up separate national centers, as in Mali.

Both the referendum and Guinean efforts to retain control of an interterritorial labor movement created serious political and trade union tensions. In this situation the CGT-FO and the Croyant/Christian unions, which also had severed their formal connections with the French unions and had Africanized their cadres, looked increasingly for outside support, not only to France but also to the ICFTU, often with official encouragement. As a result, a sudden spate of new ICFTU affiliates started to crop up in French African territories. The new Western trade union interest in the area was marked by an ICFTU exploratory mission to the French-speaking Black African states of West and Equatorial Africa in the summer of 1960 and the subsequent Third African Regional Organization Conference in Tunis in November, 1960. Whereas in 1959, the ICFTU listed only one French Black African affiliate in Madagascar, during the next two and one-half years, it obtained eight additional ones. These affiliations, however, were relatively short-lived, since most of the governments in French-speaking West and Equatorial Africa imposed unification of the unions and forced them to abandon their outside international ties. In 1965, the ICFTU had only four affiliates in French-speaking Black Africa, and none in West Africa. However, in Dahomey, Senegal and Upper Volta, the united trade unions split again; or when unity was restored, the various factions retained their separate identities, enabling the Western trade unions to maintain at least indirect ties through the International Trade Secretariats and individual assistance programs of the AFL-CIO, the German DGB, and the Histadrut. Moreover, many French-speaking Black African Unions shifted their international ties from the ICFTU and AFRO to the moderate African Trade Union Confederation (ATUC), which had been formed in 1962, supported by both the ICFTU and the International Federation of Christian Trade Unions (IFCTU).

ICFTU REGIONALISM AND THE PAN-AFRICAN LABOR MOVEMENT

ICFTU policy in Africa was largely patterned by its previous experience in Latin America and Asia. There it had extended its protective alliance to various trade unions calling themselves free (as distinct from those under Communist control) against Communist labor movements which, under instructions from the Soviet Union and the local Communist parties, sought to undermine their rivals wherever possible. Even before the creation of the ICFTU, the unions in both Asia and Latin America had, with the aid of the American labor movement, formed regional alliances against strong Communist rivals, and the ICFTU inherited these regional organizations.[10] Moreover, the ICFTU came on the scene only after most of these countries had received their independence. These two sets of circumstances help to explain why, despite the many difficulties of the Latin-American and Asian unions with the ICFTU and its leading Western affiliates, there was no stampede toward disaffiliation comparable to that in Africa.

The ICFTU demonstrated its first serious interest in the

---

[10]The Asian Federation of Labor became the forerunner of the Asian Regional Organization (ARO) and the Inter-American Regional Organization (ORIT) of the ICFTU.

labor movements of Black Africa in 1953 with the establishment of information offices in Accra and Nairobi, both manned by British trade unionists. Earlier several ICFTU missions had visited Africa to make contacts with trade union leaders, nationalists, and colonial authorities, and in 1951, a West African Regional Conference and seminar were conducted in Douala, Cameroon. Until the Suez crisis in late 1956, the training, advisory and other support activities of the ICFTU remained largely extensions of activities conducted by the TUC, usually in cooperation with colonial authorities. The failure of the colonial powers to shore up their waning political influence militarily, in the face of U.S. and Soviet opposition, proved the watershed in the African decolonization process and led to a radical tactical and operational change of the ICFTU's African program.

The first open association of the ICFTU with African regionalism occurred at its First African Regional Conference in Accra in January, 1957, immediately after the Suez crisis. The conference coincided with the establishment of UGTAN and was timed to mark the impending independence of Ghana, the first British colony to obtain its freedom. That same year, the ICFTU held its Fifth World Congress in Tunis to demonstrate its solidarity with the aspiration of the Afro-Asian movements. At both meetings the ICFTU, under AFL-CIO initiative, made clear that it would no longer be restricted to the cautious policies initiated by the unions from the colonial powers, especially the TUC. Henceforth, it would conduct an aggressive anti-colonialist policy supporting trade unions as well as political aspirations of the Africans. This policy shift provoked sharp clashes with the British and French unions over the role and responsibilities of the International, warnings that excessive zeal in gaining affiliates might endanger the unity of African unions, opposition to subsidizing unstable national federations, and charges that the Americans lacked understanding of the political problems in the African colonies. Not only did the British and French still smart under their failure at Suez, but the French were fighting a rebellion in Algeria, and the British faced the Mau Mau emergency in Kenya. However, despite British fears, TUC opposition remained largely limited to complaints and the delay of contributions.

To carry out this new and more aggressive program, the Tunis Congress established an International Solidarity Fund through which the wealthier unions in the advanced countries could finance aid to the unions in the colonial countries without requiring an increase of affiliation fees for the others. The separate administration of this fund by the donors was to end the proliferation of independent activities outside the ICFTU. But for that it was already too late; and when the Americans refused to abandon their own programs, the Germans, Israelis and others followed suit.

Under the banner of anticolonialist militancy for which the AFL-CIO now set the tone, the financially strengthened ICFTU sought to accommodate within its own framework the growing regional nationalist and separatist sentiments of the Africans by offering to establish an African Regional Organization to be run by the Africans themselves. Warnings by the TUC General Secretary that the Africans had neither the administrative nor financial resources to operate such an organization were disregarded as prejudiced. As the transition of the African countries to independence gained momentum, so did the membership of the ICFTU, which at its 1962 congress could claim thirty African affiliates, nearly double the 1957 number. During their respective independence campaigns, such diverse nationalist leaders as Mboya, Nkrumah, Nyerere, Kaunda, Ferhat Abbas and Bourguiba had availed themselves of the services of the ICFTU and had praised it for its contribution to their national causes.

By 1962, the trend toward disaffiliation from the ICFTU was well under way, having started with the Ghana TUC's withdrawal at the end of 1959; however, a number of increasingly neutralist and anti-Western labor movements in the nonaligned camp retained some links with the Western trade unions through the International Trade Secretariats. But by 1965, the number of African ICFTU affiliates had dwindled to sixteen, several of them insignificant, in exile, or on the verge of disaffiliation, as African governments increasingly forced unions to abandon their international ties, or as some unions chose to disaffiliate because of internal disunity or domestic political considerations. The tide of formal international affiliation had irreversibly turned, and the Western unions were forced to maintain contacts with the Africans by less formal means.

THE CONFRONTATION IN AFRICA

The importance of the ICFTU as a political symbol for the

Africans--which, of course, also determined its usefulness as a technical assistance agency--was mainly related to decolonization. Once this was achieved, Communism and Soviet intervention failed to replace colonialism as the main threat, and competing efforts of the most radical African nationalist spokesmen to establish a new African regional identity through Pan-African movements made it increasingly difficult for Western trade unions to subordinate African regionalism to the cause of "international free trade unionism." Even the most partisan pro-ICFTU leaders in Africa became more and more equivocal about their commitments to Brussels, ICFTU headquarters, and tried to avoid any initiative in breaking all ties with the Pan-African AATUF until they were forced to do so on the insistence of its General Secretary, John Tettegah. However, unlike the Africans, the ICFTU had no choice but to be hostile to the AATUF. Since the efforts to form the African Regional Organization (AFRO) coincided with the birth of the Pan-African labor movement--first UGTAN in 1957 and then AATUF in 1961--the two tendencies were bound to clash.[11]

In confrontation with Pan-Africanism, AFRO became a protective association arrayed against a more militant nationalist and separatist African movement which sought to exploit the trade unions on behalf of the more aggressive African states, especially the Casablanca powers.[12] Since the trade union campaign sponsored by these states also obtained support from the Communist camp through the WFTU and individual Communist unions, the Western trade unions sought to structure and justify their African alliance in Cold War terms. This effort was partially successful, and the alliance grew and held together as long as much of the continent was still in transition toward independence. But the issue of an African *versus* a pro-Western international alliance became increasingly sensitive, intensifying rivalries with other movements as well as internal strains among affiliates.

Once independence was no longer a regional problem, the governments and ruling parties began to sort out their internal

---

[11] AFRO was formally established at the Third African Regional Conference of the ICFTU in Tunis in November, 1960.

[12] The Casablanca powers were the United Arab Republic (UAR), Ghana, Guinea, Mali, Algeria and Morocco.

and external alliances and offered the trade unions clientele relations in return for acquiescence and political loyalty. At this stage the formal system of alliance with the Western trade unions began to break down in an increasing number of countries. Significantly, with the breakdown of the ICFTU and AFRO as the leading trade union alliance in Africa, the two rival Pan-African labor movements--AATUF, representing the Casablanca powers and especially Ghanaian aspirations to regional domination, and ATUC, representing the Monrovia powers' interests at the trade union level--also declined in importance.[13] Their mutual rivalry impeded their efforts to structure their respective alliances; nor could they overcome the conflicts which also beset the Organization of African Unity (OAU). Moreover, despite some subsidies, they lacked the resources of the ICFTU and the WFTU.

INTERNATIONALISM AND INTERNAL CONFLICTS

The difficulties of the Western trade unions to continue formal alliances with the African unions despite considerable expenditures of personnel, money and educational efforts, can be attributed not only to international power relations, but also to internal conflicts which assumed increasingly ideological forms and therefore took on Cold War implications. In these struggles, some rival trade union groups and factions appealed for support to the ICFTU and its major affiliates; others to the AATUF and its allies and sponsors--including the WFTU, bloc trade unions and governments, and the governments of Ghana and the United Arab Republic. By taking sides, the outside forces became committed to those whom they aided, but with little or no commitments from them in return. The main hope of each side was that a victory of its allies would deny the other influence detrimental to its larger interests and prestige. Thus the Cold War aspect of internal conflicts became somewhat synthetic.

---

[13]The Monrovia states included the moderate French-speaking Black African states plus such others as Liberia, Nigeria, Sierra Leone, and Ethiopia.

In these contests the stakes of the ICFTU were considerably larger than those of its rivals. Influenced by Western training and trade union principles as well as a Western-type industrial relations system inherited from the colonial administrations, many African union leaders thus became committed to the doctrine of trade union autonomy from political parties and governments. As these men watched the growing trend of government and party intervention in the name of "African Socialism" and the replacement of old leaders by nationalist militants, some tried to withdraw from party politics, and others threatened or tried to break with the dominant political movements (as in Tanzania, Uganda, Zambia, Rhodesia, Nigeria and Ghana). Furthermore, faced with rigid wage controls imposed from above and discontent in their ranks over economic, social and tribal inequities, as well as corruption, arrogance and waste in government, these union leaders felt compelled to demonstrate their ability to protest. When the governments reacted, often in heavy-handed fashion, the unions appealed to the ICFTU or the ITS for support and comfort, thereby compromising even old and cordial relations between international trade union officials and government leaders, who in self-defense raised the issue of outside intervention.

The more the ICFTU expended effort and money to shore up its alliance in Africa and to help its friends and affiliates, the more the anti-Western labor groups sought compensatory support from bloc and Ghanaian sources in the name of anti-imperialism and anticolonialism. Since such contacts and support were often clandestine and informal and carried out in the name of African nationalism, they became much less vulnerable to charges of foreign intervention than aid to the pro-ICFTU unions. Even where government action against foreign ties was intended to be impartial, it hurt the pro-ICFTU forces more than the others, since openly given Western aid could be more easily stopped than the hidden aid of the AATUF-WFTU forces. The objective of radical labor groups and their allies was to discredit the ICFTU-aligned labor elements and the ICFTU in order to force a break of their ties, either through government intervention or through a revolt against the leadership. By depriving the old leadership of its foreign subsidies for maintaining trade union facilities and services, as well as patronage, the radical elements sought to capture the organization.

Although maneuvers to change the trade union leadership from below often failed, in the ensuing struggles many unions divided, reunited temporarily during domestic crises, and split again. Some labor leaders, afraid of party interventions with their leadership, turned against their erstwhile political allies and mentors and tried to assert the principles of trade union autonomy. Others sought vainly to translate their labor following into political movements. But generally, such challenges of political movements were unsuccessful and weakened the unions.[14]

The contest for outside assistance and personal ties continues, even where formal alignments have been broken. For those successful in gaining international attention, it is a status symbol giving them access to the political scene, enabling them to publicize themselves and their movements and to acquire prestige far beyond their indigenous trade union resources. This also affords satisfaction to their foreign allies, constituting a measure of the latter's success in influencing and strengthening friendly trade unions and thereby impressing also the political groups with which their labor protégés are allied. Here, of course, the ICFTU and the Western trade unions were mainly interested in protecting and enlarging their allied movements; if necessary, by helping them shift their emphasis from traditional but politically risky protest and industrial relations functions to primarily social welfare functions.

In contrast, the more militant labor camp demanded radical changes in the whole political and economic system, for which it sought support from the bloc and the AATUF. Its

---

[14] To be noted in this connection are the considerable stability of the unions and the loyalty of the workers to their elected union leaders, which as the East African examples have shown, make it difficult for the labor movements to be captured through mere bribery and political manipulation. Nor have the African governments found it easy to impose controls upon their trade unions. The workers are able to differentiate their trade union and political loyalties with remarkable consistency. After all, it took strong police measures to bring the Tanzanian unions to heel, and even then, when the virtually emasculated labor movement threatened to fall apart, the government had to make concessions to its leaders. Kenya offers another example of the difficulty of imposing party control over the selection of the trade union leadership.

leaders hoped to use the trade unions as centers for establishing extraparliamentary alliances through which their friends and sympathizers in and outside government can bring about a transformation of the system. But in the absence of adequate political and organizational strength for engendering such internal changes, they pressed for shifts in foreign policy. This coincided more with the interests of their foreign sponsors, whose encouragement of internal pressures was related more to diplomacy than to the principles of revolution.

As the African governments became increasingly concerned with the divisive and corruptive influence of much of the international labor activities, some decided to impose unity on the unions and to prohibit international affiliations or restrict them to African regional ties. These measures were usually invoked in the name of African Socialism and as part of the unification process of the body politic through one-party systems and nonalignment. While some countries, such as Guinea, Mali, Ghana, and Tanzania, used this to exclude virtually all Western trade union contacts, others continued to tolerate such contacts as long as they did not involve formal ties. Among the latter were Kenya, Zambia, and Senegal.

A few governments still permit unrestricted international affiliations, as, for instance, Nigeria and the Democratic Republic of the Congo (Leopoldville). Ethiopia now looks mainly to the ICFTU and the American labor movement for assistance in building up its infant trade unions. Tolerance for retaining formal or informal contacts with the Western trade unions serves to reassure the business community and the Western powers, avoids weakening one segment of the labor movement at the expense of another, and becomes a form of patronage. Moreover, some governments are aware that complete cuts of outside aid may deprive union leaders of prestige and training opportunities. Thus ITS activities and bilateral assistance programs of the AFL-CIO and its African-American Labor Center, the German DGB and its Friedrich Ebert Stiftung, as well as the Histadrut and its Afro-Asian Institute, the Austrian OGB, and the Swiss unions continue to be widely accepted in Africa as substitutes for former ICFTU ties and assistance.

Henceforth, the ICFTU will continue to operate in the few countries in which trade union rivalries have not been resolved or where governments are anxious to obtain "respectable" outside assistance for their moderate trade unions. In the meantime, the rivalry over international alignment shifted to the AATUF *versus* the ATUC. However, since these two movements lacked the resources of the ICFTU or WFTU, on whom they continued to be partially dependent, the conflict was reduced to a somewhat lower key.

THE COMMUNISTS AND
THE PAN-AFRICAN LABOR MOVEMENT

Originally, the WFTU, as a united front movement, had tried to recruit as many African unions as possible with the aid of its British and French affiliates. Soon after it split in 1949, it lost interest in including non-Communist unions in its ranks. A few Communists in Ghana, Sierre Leone, and Nigeria received financial assistance from the WFTU and the French CGT and sought to affiliate their unions with the WFTU, but their petitions seem to have been held in abeyance. The Sudan was the only British territory in which the WFTU had a significant Communist-led affiliate. In 1951, the WFTU rejected the idea of establishing in Africa and Asia regional organizations patterned after the ICFTU.

Instead of promoting African affiliates in the absence of Communist parties, it decided to avoid questions of ideological divergence and guidance by establishing united front or tactical relations on the basis of anticolonialism and anti-imperialism. Although the Communists and the WFTU leaders stressed common ideological ties with the African nationalists based on anti-imperialism, anticapitalism, and a common faith in "socialist" solutions of internal and international problems, they considered that ultimately the nationalist ambitions of the Africans and Afro-Asians might clash with the universalist ideology of Communism. Furthermore, African nationalist and bloc priorities in international relations could not always be presumed to coincide, thus making impractical the formal inclusion of African nationalist movements in the Communist club of the WFTU. "Nonalignment," as a process of detachment of the merging African states from their Western ties, adequately served Soviet efforts to break out of diplomatic isolation.

As the African anti-Western and socialist clamor became increasingly militant, the Communists tried to accommodate African ideology within their universalist framework by proclaiming the possibility of bypassing capitalism in the development of pre-capitalist societies toward socialism. Those friendliest to the bloc were declared "National Democracies," a new pre-socialist stage of social development, and international Communist journals publicized African claims that the class struggle did not apply to African societies, and that all opposition to "National Democratic" governments and to Pan-African unity was criminal, serving the purpose of the imperialists.

These accommodations of the African nationalists, together with bloc offers of aid, proved highly successful in earning credit for the Soviet Union as a factor in decolonization and as a power with substantial African interests. In building these relations, the Soviets showed little concern for the fate of indigenous Communist parties or unions and gave little encouragement to individual Communists or groups seeking to set up new parties or unions which could disturb official relations and challenge the "nonaligned" commitments and unity tendencies of the African nationalists. Since 1956, the WFTU has been quite willing to abandon most of its African affiliates and to induce them, with the aid of the Communist unions and parties of the metropolitan countries, which retained guiding responsibilities, to merge with the nationalist unions. At the international level, the WFTU stressed unity of action and demonstrated solidarity with the Africans on such issues as Algerian independence, South African racism, Rhodesia, Portuguese colonialism and U.S. intervention in the Congo.

Perhaps more important than joint meetings on these issues were the increasing support and assistance which the WFTU and individual bloc unions gave to the Pan-African labor movement, first to the UGTAN under Guinean sponsorship, and then to the largely Ghana-controlled AATUF, which was established in May, 1961, at Casablanca. The opening of the AATUF Congress was the high-water mark of Pan-African labor solidarity. After much bickering and many preliminary meetings, it brought together African unions of all international and ideological tendencies to form a federation and draw up common principles in a Pan-African labor charter. The ICFTU, the

WFTU, the Christian IFCTU, and the Pan-Arab ICATU were all represented by observers. In drawing up the AATUF Constitution the most militant Pan-African spokesmen, especially from Ghana, Guinea, and the United Arab Republic, insisted on a clause requiring all members to disaffiliate from any other international except the ICATU.

Since the Constitution Committee was dominated by representatives of unions from the Casablanca powers, their insistence on disaffiliation prevailed. The only concession made to the pro-ICFTU and IFCTU unions was a ten-month period of grace for disaffiliation and the establishment of AATUF headquarters in Casablanca, where the UMT, itself an ICFTU affiliate, offered to keep it from falling under control of its Ghanaian General Secretary, John Tettegah. Confronted with this ultimatum, the ICFTU and the Christian unions, which had the majority of organizations but probably not of total membership, walked out rather than risk a vote on the floor of the conference or a polemic on Pan-African solidarity. Subsequently, they charged, with some justice, that the representation of their opponents in the conference and the Constitution Committee had been rigged by a hostile conference management.

Such was the appeal of Pan-Africanism that even a year later, when the moderate unions established their own African Trade Union Confederation (ATUC) at Dakar, they still left the door open for eventual unity. However, they insisted on the right to choose their outside affiliation, the denial of which they considered an abrogation of their autonomy and a threat to their existence. They also appealed to the ICFTU and the IFCTU to support the ATUC as an alternative to their own African regional organizations and to make the ICFTU College in Kampala and the former IFCTU School in Brazzaville available to them. But as long as AFRO and the Pan-African Union of Believing Workers (UPIC) were held together by the substantial resources of the ICFTU and the IFCTU, with the first concentrating on the English- and the latter on the French-speaking areas, the internationals gave little assistance. Without their substantial aid, ATUC found it difficult to overcome the difference between its dominant French affiliates and those of the English-speaking areas, or between the East, West, and North African subregional groups. Its other handicaps were lack of credibility as a militant nationalist Pan-African movement, and ICFTU-IFCTU rivalries and preoccupations with their own members, which prevented closer collaboration in support of ATUC. Only with the virtual collapse of AFRO did the Western unions show a new interest in ATUC, as became apparent at its Lagos Congress in October, 1965.

After the Casablanca Congress, the growing African anxiety over the Congo crisis and agitation for a confrontation with the white-controlled southern part of Africa made it difficult for both sides to shut the door completely to negotiations. Not only did the Western-aligned unions continue to offer negotiations despite AATUF provocations, but the AATUF unions also delayed making a final decision on the disaffiliation issue until their Second Congress, in Bamako in June, 1964. A number of key AATUF unions, such as the Moroccan UMT and the Algerian UGTA, had retained their ICFTU membership well beyond the ten-month limit stipulated at Casablanca, and even then their disaffiliation seemed not to be directly related to the AATUF decision. Even some Ghanaian unions delayed disaffiliation from the ICFTU-aligned ITS, and some UAR unions continued their membership.

In this sparring among the African unions the WFTU saw a double tactical opportunity. For one thing, it could help to undermine the ICFTU in Africa by aiding an African regional movement whose main purpose was to fight its Western rival in the name of anti-imperialism. For another, it could associate itself with the unsatisfied ambitions for regional leadership of the African states most determined to intervene in the affairs of their less anti-Western neighbors, thereby contributing to the anxieties of the Western powers.

To bolster the prestige and activities of the aggressive Pan-African labor movement, the WFTU established a trade union training school first in Conakry and then in Bamako, and, according to knowledgeable ICFTU sources, increasingly subsidized the activities of the AATUF General Secretary, John Tettegah. He dispensed these funds, and subsidies from the Ghanaian Government, to organizations fighting ICFTU affiliates, as in Nigeria; to factions within movements seeking alignment with the AATUF against majority sentiment; and to individuals seeking to promote new unions against established pro-ICFTU organizations, as in Uganda and Kenya, or to subvert nonaligned movements as in Zambia, Sierra Leone and Senegal. Paralleling this AATUF campaign, the WFTU sought to strengthen its own leverage on the African labor scene and its alliance with the AATUF from below by supplementing AATUF aid with its own money and gifts, distributed to AATUF unions and sympathetic labor leaders.

The main significance of the AATUF was symbolic as the first and most militant Pan-African trade union alliance, whose affiliates were all united in their opposition to the ICFTU, the rival ATUC, and various, but not necessarily all Western trade union assistance activities. While the AATUF assumed the appearance of great strength by presumptuously claiming credit for the decline of the ICFTU in Africa, this image was deceptive and its ranks were far from solidly united. It also suffered from interregional rivalries, especially between East and West Africa and North and Sub-Saharan Africa. By admission of its own leaders, none of its affiliates made regular financial contributions. Nor did it have training or technical facilities to substitute for those provided by the ICFTU and IFCTU. At best, it could obtain for its protégés some training opportunities in the bloc through the WFTU, or in Guinea. Its Secretariat, which was moved in 1964 from Casablanca to Accra, appeared to be operating autonomously with bloc, Ghanaian Government, and such other subsidies as the ingenious John Tettegah could solicit. He, himself, did not hide his connection with the Ghanaian Foreign Office and his reliance on Ghanaian labor attachés as his eyes and ears, and as contact men. Few of the other African trade union leaders approved of Tettegah's activities or were eager to cooperate with the Ghanaians in subverting and exploiting trade union rivalries in other countries. Despite announcements of the impending establishment of an AATUF office in Lagos early in 1965, this failed to open, and the long delayed Dar es Salaam office was put completely under Tanzanian control to serve mainly local exile groups.

Most of the other co-sponsors of the AATUF, such as the Guineans, the Algerians, Malians, Moroccans and Egyptians, lost interest in using trade union contacts for other than solidarity demonstrations; Ghana was almost alone among African countries in using such contacts to intervene in the internal affairs of other African countries. The absence of a Ghanaian delegation at the October, 1965, WFTU Congress in Warsaw and the WFTU's admitted cut in expenditures raised the possibility that the bloc was losing interest in supporting Ghana's ambitions in the African labor field. One may speculate whether this estrangement was due to pressures from other African unions with which the WFTU and the bloc unions maintain relations, or to fears that support of the Ghanaian Government's ambitions might interfere with the bloc's diplomatic campaign in Africa.

Despite this apparently diminishing interest of the WFTU in Africa, bloc unions continue to maintain contacts wherever possible, and offer increased training opportunities to African labor leaders. The Soviets are obviously concerned with the competing efforts of the All-China Federation of Trade Unions (ACFTU), which has made overtures to unions in Zanzibar and Brazzaville, as well as to the National Union of Tanganyikan Workers (NUTA), the Ghana TUC, and the AATUF. Chinese Communist competition in the labor field seems so far only a minor threat, but as the Soviet Union and the WFTU are increasingly identified with the status quo and "peaceful coexistence," China has become the symbol of radical change with which the most militant and frustrated African political elements can identify themselves, and which affords them the greatest provocative utility in international relations.

GHANA AND THE AATUF

Ghana's ambitions in the labor field related to its efforts to assert itself as the leading state in a Pan-African federation and as the guiding force in the creation of a revolutionary "African ideology." In line with this objective, it sought to have the OAU and the African Regional Conference of the ILO accredit the AATUF as the sole Pan-African trade union movement. But in both of these objectives it failed. Until the military coup, which ended Nkrumah's regime in February, 1966, the AATUF tried to create the impression of vast open and clandestine support and of involvements in nearly all trade union rivalries. Part of this game of mythmaking was the rushing of an AATUF representative to the Sudan when the Communist trade unions emerged as an important factor in the overthrow of the military regime in October, 1964, in order to identify the movement with revolutionary forces wherever possible. Both the attention and the threat of this revolutionary posture were to entice or cajole unions into joining.

Tettegah's contacts with African trade unions seemed to be built mainly on individuals loyal to him and sympathetic to Ghanaian aspirations. Formal affiliations were important as a symbol of alignment with a more militant Pan-Africanism than that of the ATUC but did not necessarily make unions accessible to Ghanaian influence. Therefore, AATUF assistance generally passed through individuals who often withheld at least part of it for their personal enrichment.[15]

In such cases the AATUF had only recourse to compromising its contacts through exposures of its gifts. But such exposures, whether they came from the AATUF itself or from its enemies, rarely embarrassed Tettegah or his associates. Exposures of their labor activities and union financing were repeatedly published in Nigeria, Zambia, Kenya and Uganda. In Uganda, Tettegah's interference on the trade union scene led to a temporary rupture with the dissident Federation of Uganda Trade Unions (FUTU), which, in turn, had broken from the ICFTU-affiliated Uganda Trade Union Congress with AATUF financial help and the support of the Ministry of Labor.[16]

Beyond these efforts to orient the majority of African trade unions toward Ghanaian leadership, the AATUF also became an instrument for probing the internal as well as international political alliances in the crisis-ridden African states, and for encouraging pro-AATUF trade union groups and pro-Ghana political elements, either in the ruling parties or among opposition groups, to work more closely together. Here, as in other cases of foreign assistance to African labor leaders, AATUF money provided local labor leaders with greater political maneuverability and avenues of influence to political leaders. But in the atmosphere of African intrigues, such activities were difficult to conceal. By and large they did little more than divide the union ranks, but there remained always the possibility that individual country crises or major regional crises, such as the possible beginning of a military or guerrilla

---

[15] Allegedly some of these funds are to be invested by recipients in order to generate local funds to support political activities.

[16] Return of FUTU to the AATUF was related to the power struggle in Uganda in which the Labor Minister, a patron of FUTU, was dismissed and the union leadership changed.

phase in the confrontation with South Africa and Rhodesia, could produce enough of a sense of community to create a united Pan-African political alliance paralleled by a Pan-African labor movement. In 1963, the concern over increasing Western involvement in the Congo crisis and the establishment of the OAU nearly produced continental trade union unity.

But subsequently this spirit of unity declined, and, by March, 1966, it seemed far removed. The fall of Nkrumah and the dismantlement of his party and trade union apparatus has removed Ghana as the gadfly of Pan-Africanism. For the time being this will very likely depolarize the African trade union alliances and relax hostile pressures in several African states against Western trade union assistance. But the recent wave of African coups does not presage any significant reversal of the trend toward disaffiliation from either the International Confederaation of Free Trade Unions (ICFTU) or the World Federation of Trade Unions (WFTU). The Conference of African Labor Ministers in Accra, January 31 to February 4, 1966, clearly indicated the mounting wariness among African political and labor leaders against being stampeded into supporting a Ghana-dominated and OAU-accredited Pan-African labor movement whose membership was made conditional on relinquishing all formal international ties and on submitting even informal international activities to the scrutiny and possible censorship of John Tettegah, the Ghanaian General Secretary of the All-African Trade Union Federation (AATUF). This was a matter of policy affecting not only trade union autonomy but governmental policy as well.

CONCLUSION

Currently Soviet bloc trade unions and the WFTU, no less than the Western trade unions and the ICFTU and IFCTU, have taken a somewhat more sober view of their relations with the African trade unions. They are bothered by what they regard as an excessively parochial preoccupation with African affairs and lack of understanding that assistance by foreign trade unions requires mutual involvement and a sense of reciprocal obligations, because it has to be justified by the donors to their own constituent members. Moreover, with independence, foreign trade union concern with political and social injustice in Africa diminished and seems to have been replaced by a sense of fatigue resulting from the Africans' demands to see not only their own problems, but world problems through African eyes--as they have done in the ILO. Nevertheless, Africa with all its problems poses both a fascination and a challenge to the outsiders who have become involved with it, be it on the governmental or the trade union level. Thus, while the status of trade union internationals in Africa has little meaning, national trade unions, with the assistance and encouragement of their governments, are assuming the burden of aiding the African unions.

However, the halcyon days of foreign trade union assistance seem to be passing and the African trade unions will increasingly have to look to internal sources and institutions for help, support and training. Chief among these will be the political parties, the labor ministries, the educational systems, and the expatriate employers and technicians who continue in many countries to exercise considerable influence on the development of industrial relations. Their interest in the establishment of effective industrial relations in Africa is far more immediate than that of any outsider. Yet this is also one of the most difficult and urgent institutional requirements. African experiments with political and administrative restrictions on trade unions have so far proved rather unsatisfactory, especially given the lack of trained administrators and the precarious power balances that exist even within one-party systems. Needs in Africa remain tremendous, and the Western trade unions, with all their past assistance in training and organizing, guiding and contributing money, have barely made a dent.

Although the African governments are exceedingly sensitive to the protest function of the trade unions, this remains an essential role for labor and for the urban proletariat. Neglect or suppression of the unions by an inefficient and corrupt administration and by heavy-handed resort to police may have long-range implications for the security and stability of the new African countries. Protest has a strange way of emerging in various forms. If labor and other interest groups are prevented from carrying out their normal functions, protest may, for instance, assume more traditional African forms of tribal or apocalyptic religious rebellions, or it may throw the unions into alliance with the military forces.

CHAPTER 9   EURAFRICANISM:
IMPACT ON AFRICAN LABOR

Willard A. Beling †

Provoking a variety of African conferences, alliances and counteralliances since 1958, Pan-Africanism has contributed a large section to the relatively huge literature that has been published in the meantime on African politics. Eurafricanism is comparatively untreated, on the other hand, particularly in the more popular works on contemporary Africa. In contrast to Pan-Africanism, for example, Eurafricanism has failed to generate scarcely a paperback title. It rarely commands a chapter even in some of the serious studies of African politics, frequently little more than a passing reference.

Although the origins of Pan-Africanism go back in a sense to the first Pan-African Conference held in London in 1900, Pan-Africanism in its presently accepted meaning can be traced to the All African Peoples Conference held in Accra in 1958. Responding in large measure to Dr. Kwame Nkrumah's leadership and articulation of the concept, Pan-Africanism henceforth became a vehicle of truly monolithic continental aspirations. Keeping pace with these developments, a Pan-African mystique naturally evolved. A number of writers on Africa have treated

---

†Willard A. Beling is Professor of International Relations and Coordinator of the Middle East/North African Program at the University of Southern California; Consulting Associate of the International Institute for Labour Studies (Geneva, 1966-68); and Editor of the *Maghreb Digest*. His most recent relevant publications are *Pan-Arabism and Labor* (1960); *Modernization and African Labor: A Tunisian Case Study* (1965); and a number of articles in scholarly journals. He is the editor of this volume and co-editor of a forthcoming volume on *The Dynamics of Development: Institutions, Processes and Techniques.*

the mythbuilding character of concepts such as the *African Personality, Negritude* and *African Socialism.*

In the meantime, Eurafricanism had also become a reality. Seeking a cause-and-effect relationship between it and Pan-Africanism, one might assume that Eurafricanism, as an obvious antithesis to Pan-Africanism, had in fact arisen as an opposing force to it. But on the contrary, Eurafricanism preceded Pan-Africanism in time and had, at least in part, provoked Pan-Africanism's initial development. In a larger measure, it shaped Pan-Africanism's subsequent orientation.

It is a thesis of this chapter that Eurafricanism has quietly grown in the meantime at the expense of Pan-Africanism. But although Eurafricanism had already achieved its ascendancy by 1963, it is still not all-embracing. Pockets of outright opposition, or indifference, still remain. For the most part, however, they are now unrelated to organized Pan-Africanism which, in fact, has become moribund. On the other hand, Eurafricanism remains a paramount African political concern.

Writers on the Pan-African labor movement have, for the most part, treated its responses to the international scene within the context of the Cold War. It is the thesis of the author, however, that Pan-African labor's responses must be evaluated also within the framework of Eurafricanism. Within these parameters, its responses have often had the merit of being logical even though unacceptable, quite naturally, to the European labor movements. They in turn helped form the attitudes of the American labor movement. Interested primarily in Cold War issues in Africa--at least until recently--the latter considered Eurafricanism as merely an important ancillary to the all-embracing Western defense system against international Communism's inroads into Africa. Recognizing in the meantime all the implications of Eurafricanism, the American labor movement has begun to alter its approach to Africa.

As Dorothy Nelkin has pointed out earlier (in Chapter 7), African labor unity was to be both the precursor and the major building block of continental unity. The Pan-African labor movement, of course, was not a purely *sui generic* labor movement. The major proponents of all-embracing African political unity, Kwame Nkrumah and Sekou Touré, as is well known, were the early proponents of Pan-African labor unity and continued to play important roles in the Pan-African labor movement. While the continental labor groupings have been in reality paper organizations, as Dorothy Nelkin correctly characterizes them, the Pan-African labor movement has nevertheless been the most functionally successful of all Pan-African organizations to date. Its spokesmen and documentation also articulate Pan-African positions perhaps more clearly and consistently than those of any other Pan-African organization. (When the author indicates a Pan-African position in the following pages, one may correctly assume that this is Pan-African labor's position.) For all these reasons, therefore, the impact of Eurafricanism on Pan-African labor and its responses are of particular interest.

EURAFRICANISM

While a loosely knit American community of interests linking North America and Latin America has roots in history going back at least as far as the Monroe Doctrine, Eurafricanism as a *community* concept is a relatively recent phenomenon. In an interesting treatment of the origins of Eurafricanism, Professor McKay traces the concept to the 1920's.[1] Writing in this early period, for example, a Frenchman formulated an interesting hypothesis which, in modified form, has been advocated in recent years in Europe, but particularly by the French[2] and the Germans. Employing an ingenious geopolitical division of the world into longitudinal sections, Eugène Guernier noted that there are three logical intercontinental communities-- Eurafrica, Asia-Australia and the Americas.[3] Arguing that latitudinal exchanges of dissimilar products were illogical because of their similarity due to comparable climates, he suggested that longitudinal (that is, North-South) exchange of dis-

---

[1] Vernon McKay, *Africa in World Politics* (New York; Harper & Row, 1963).

[2] An articulate advocate of Eurafricanism, for example, Professor François Perroux is Director of the Institut de Science Appliquée; Director of the Institut d'Etude du Développement Economique et Social (with its well-known journal *Tiers Monde)*; and member of the Conseil Economique et Social.

[3] *L'Afrique-Champ d'Expansion de l'Europe* (Paris, 1933), pp. 271-78.

similar products is the natural arrangement. In effect, these longitudinal divisions provide three self-sufficient communities.

As a practical concept, however, Eurafricanism became a reality only in 1957, when the European Six negotiated the Treaty of Rome for the establishment of the European Common Market that went into effect on January 1, 1959. Those that were still African colonial powers brought their overseas territories into the community. But stated somewhat more broadly than this, the Treaty of Rome provided for the association of "non-European countries and territories which have special relations with Belgium, France, Italy and the Netherlands."[4] Provisions were thus also made for former colonial territories of these specific countries.

Within this framework, African states with French relations would obviously predominate. Thus, the states composing the Union Africaine et Malgache (UAM) became the core of the African associates of EEC. Beginning essentially as a grouping of twelve former French colonies that were closely tied to France, they announced the establishment of UAM in March, 1961. In the following September, they formally organized the union in a meeting in Tanarive of the Malagasy Republic, an island lying off the eastern coast of Africa. Somewhat enlarged, the UAM has regrouped in the meantime as the Organization Commune Africaine et Malgache (OCAM). Added to this core of French-related states, there were three former Belgian colonies and Somalia which, in fact, was a union of a former Italian territory and a British colony. As of the end of 1965, these African associates of the EEC were known as the "Eighteen."[5]

The Common Market did not include Britain, Portugal and Spain, of course, each of which also had African territories. Excluded from the Common Market and from its development of the Eurafrican community, Britain nevertheless has had its own

---

[4] Treaty of Rome, Articles 131-36 and Annex IV.
[5] Burundi, the Federal Republic of Cameroon, the Central African Republic, Chad, the Congo Republic (Brazzaville), the Republic of the Congo (Leopoldville), the Ivory Coast, Dahomey, Gabon, Upper Volta, Mali, the Islamic Republic of Mauritania, Niger, Rwanda, Senegal, the Republic of Somalia, Togo and the Malagasy Republic.

interests in Africa. Operating perforce within the framework of the European Free Trade Association (EFTA) or "Outer Seven," as well as that of the Commonwealth, Britain hoped to retain her African ties and the concomitant advantages.

Involving herself in technical aid and assistance programs both alone and with other governments interested in African development, including the members of EEC, for example, Britain has moved in the direction of regional economic integration. Indeed, the so-called East African Common Market historically has roots that antedate those of the Union Africaine et Malgache. For deriving from the British East African High Commission, the East African Common Service Organization (EACSO) emerged when the states became independent. Embracing Kenya, Uganda and Tanzania, EACSO constitutes in essence an East African "Common Market."[6]

Making its bid for entry into the Common Market in the meantime, Britain made it conditional on its former colonies' enjoying the same privileges that the former possessions of the European Six enjoy. While the other European states of the EEC were in favor from the beginning of enlarging the base to allow the anglophonic states to associate on equal terms-- particularly Germany, which had no African ties and felt itself at a distinct disadvantage, particularly to France in Africa-- France did not favor the concept.

Failing itself in its bid to join the EEC in 1963, Britain's former possessions were thereafter allowed to apply for association with the EEC. But with the exception of Sierra Leone, all the anglophonic states openly rejected the possibility. In the meantime, however, serious negotiations for an association agreement with Nigeria--earlier a sharp critic of African association--were designed to make it the first of its kind with a Commonwealth country.

---

[6]Benton F. Massell, *East African Economic Union: An Evaluation and Some Implications for Policy*, a Memorandum (Santa Monica: The Rand Corporation, n. d.); IBRD, *The Economic Development of Uganda* (Baltimore: John Hopkins Press, 1962); Joseph S. Nye, Jr., "East Africa: From Common Market to Federation," *Africa Report*, Vol. VIII, No. 8 (August, 1963), pp. 3-6; Carl G. Rosberg and Aaron Segal,"An East African Federation," *International Conciliation*, No. 543 (1963).

SEEDS OF CONFLICT IN EURAFRICANISM

A conflict between Pan-Africanism and Eurafricanism was almost unavoidable in view of Africa's historical development. Dominated for years by European colonial powers, for example, the Africans rushed during the past decade or so to sever their colonial ties with Europe so that, with the exception of a few still pending areas at issue, all of Africa suddenly became independent. But new relationships were inevitable, not only with others but also with the former colonial powers.

The latter naturally posed the most serious problem. For most Africans were aware that the Cold War had forced some colonial powers to liberate their African holdings and others to accelerate the process. Thus it was perfectly natural that some held as a corollary that as reluctant givers of independence to African states, the former colonial powers intended to reassert colonial ties as soon as they could. Allegedly, Eurafricanism was the first step and thus should be prevented at all costs. Nevertheless, a number of Africans favored close ties with Europe in the new bilateral Eurafrican framework that promised Africa support rather than subordination and cooperation instead of coercion.

Obviously discredited now as a major force in African politics, Pan-Africanism apparently has lost out in its struggle against Eurafricanism. Nevertheless, this chapter examines the implications of Eurafricanism in terms of the Pan-African charges. For while neocolonialism may neither have been intended nor is even now apparent to some of the participants in the concept, it may indeed be an inescapable by-product of evolving Eurafricanism.

As a Marxist neologism, of course, *neocolonialism* may imply more evil than actually exists in the current Eurafrican relationship. Recalling the semantic shift in Marxist dialectic on words like "democracy," "freedom," "peace" and many others, one conceivably could defend Eurafrican neocolonialism just as some have argued that, in certain instances at least, the values of colonialism outweighed its evils. A Middle Eastern expert used to chide representatives of a certain nation in jest, for example, that they would have been several decades ahead if they had only been a British colony.

Without either supporting the charges or defending neocolonialism, the author suggests that Eurafricanism has been a major factor in shaping Pan-African labor's xenophobic orientation. The author also suggests that, although the Eurafrican issue was once a divisive issue, it is becoming the common ground, albeit unarticulated clearly as such at this point, on which new relationships between African and Western labor are being built. This becomes clearer as Franco-American, as well as Franco-British, relations become further strained.

EUROPE: PRIMUS INTER PARES

Justifiably absorbed in the national struggle for independence, African nationalists had little time (or indeed opportunity) to exercise themselves regarding the future problems of states that at best were only in embryo during most of the struggle. Africa is thus still in flux. Independence was not an end in itself. Giving the nationalists hardly a moment to catch their breath, independence forced them to face two far more difficult problems to resolve: that is, the task of nation-building, and all it implies, and the formation of foreign policy.

Independence popularly implies autonomy, freedom and sovereignty. As Napoleon once said, like honor, it is a rocky island without a beach. Moving suddenly from subordination to sovereign statehood within the space of only a few mere years, many Africans entertained at least briefly the rocky island concept. Nevertheless, independence is in fact a relative thing. No man, or country for that matter, can be an island to himself, particularly in the framework of modern international politics.

Initially, however, the newly independent African states freely exercised their new sovereignty. Formally rejecting close ties with the metropole for the postindependence period, for example, certain of the French-speaking areas made this their first expression of sovereignty even before they had attained independence. Aligning themselves then with the Soviets and/or Red Chinese, a number of former British and French colonies-- among others, Ghana, Guinea and Algeria--then underscored their sovereign rights within the framework of the Cold War.

Nevertheless, sovereignty implies equality in only a very few well-defined areas. To list but a few of the exceptions, for example, one could hardly equate Ghana and Britain or Guinea and France in a ranking of nations in terms of power. And in comparative development, of course, the disparity between Western Europe and Africa is perfectly obvious. For whatever term is applied, "developing," "emerging," or other euphemisms, African nations in general are self-admittedly underdeveloped. As a European community, the European half of the Eurafrican pairing embraces, among other things, a quasi-common defense system in NATO, a Common Market, a European Coal and Steel Community, a common atomic energy program--all of which some observers consider as the building blocks of *supra* nation-building. On the other hand, the African half of the Eurafrican match is still involved in mere nation-building.

In a real sense, Europe rather than Africa was the overriding consideration in the early conception of Eurafricanism. It was endorsed as an important factor in restoring war-devastated Europe, for example, so that it could still stand against the Soviet threat. As America provided capital to restore Europe's industry, Africa was to provide it with the raw material. Being totally European in its conception, therefore, the European emphasis was a natural development that also drew its logic from the fact that at this early stage, Europe still held most of Africa as colonial territories.

But while the rebuilding of Europe was a primary factor, Eurafricanism obviously grew out of more than economic considerations. Among other things, for example, it was to provide a means to maintain political influences in Africa where the European powers were in the process of losing, or already had lost, their colonies (as in the case of Germany). Eurafricanism was to provide, in effect, a future bulwark against Communism's encroachments in Africa that the colonial powers themselves had been able to thwart as long as they physically occupied Africa.

France's traumatic experience with Communism in Indochina, and with what many Frenchmen subsequently mistakenly considered as Communism in Algeria, made her eager to ensure continued European influence in Africa. France thus agreed to the establishment of the Common Market only on condition that the overseas territories were also admitted. Indeed, she was prepared to go it alone to build a Franco-African *communauté française*.[7] The Constantine Plan for Algeria that de Gaulle announced in 1958, calling for an expenditure of roughly $4 billion in five years was, at least in part, an expression of this determination.

As another vital consideration in the European development of Eurafricanism, World War II had demonstrated Africa's strategic importance to Europe. At almost any price, therefore, Africa had to be denied to the Soviets as a base which they could use as a springboard against Europe. But just as the European Defense Community had failed to materialize because of France's concern with its sovereignty, a proposed Eurafrican defense system was also destined to failure as the African states assumed independence and their sovereignty.

Joining forces against the threat of international Communism, the labor movements of the free world had established the International Confederation of Free Trade Unions (ICFTU) in 1949 as a counter to the Communist-dominated World Federation of Trade Unions (WFTU). Aware of the Soviet threat in Africa--the WFTU had sponsored its first Pan-African Labor Conference as early as April, 1947, in Dakar--the ICFTU began also to sponsor African labor conferences. In 1952, it succeeded in establishing a West African Advisory Committee. Deriving slowly out of these modest beginnings, the ICFTU African Regional Organization (AFRO) was formally established in 1960 in the pattern of its Asian Regional Organization (ARO) and the Inter-American Regional Organization (ORIT).[8]

That the European labor movements dominated the ICFTU

---

[7]See David C. Gordon's treatment of the French *mission civilisatrice*, their version of the "white man's burden" in their colonies, in his monograph, *North Africa's French Legacy: 1954-1962* (Cambridge: Harvard University Press, 1962), pp. 6-15.

[8]For a brief treatment of the Pan-African labor movement, see chapter nine of the author's *Modernization and African Labor*, *op. cit.*; also Jean Meynaud and Anisse Salah-Bey, *Le Syndicalisme Africain* (Paris: Payot, 1963).

at this point is an indisputable fact of history. Joining forces with the non-Europeans in 1953 at the Third ICFTU World Congress in Stockholm, in fact, the American labor movement sought to break the European control of the international movement and succeeded in mitigating it. But European paramountcy in the ICFTU, of course, is still a major issue and exercises the AFL-CIO perhaps more than other non-European affiliates, because of its size and the concomitantly large supporting financial role the American movement is called upon to bear in the ICFTU. In any case, the European affiliates of the ICFTU in its early stages considered most of Africa as still an integral part of Europe's colonial system--most of it, in fact, still was-- and, therefore, to be safeguarded like Europe itself against the Soviet threat. But colonialism was obviously doomed in the face of African nationalism and world opinion. As the concept of the EEC evolved, therefore, a built-in associational membership in it was provided to replace Europe's colonial relationships with Africa. With the exception of the Communist labor movements, European labor endorsed the EEC and African associational membership.

With hardly a glance backward, some African states immediately welcomed the establishment of a Eurafrican community. Hailing it as a "masterly concept," for example, Senegalese President Senghor indicated that his country was deeply committed to close ties between Africa and Europe.[9] Somewhat more realistic than enthusiastic, however, others have meanwhile accepted the concept reluctantly as a necessary evil in order to compete economically with those who had already associated themselves with the Eurafrican program. The Pan-African labor movement, on the other hand, remained adamantly opposed to Eurafricanism in any form.

EURAFRICANISM: EQUATED WITH NEOCOLONIALISM

The Pan-Africanists have condemned the Eurafrican concept as "neocolonialism." While a minority group that is now

---

[9] See his article, "West Africa in Evolution," *Foreign Affairs*, Vol. XXXIV, No. 2 (January, 1961), pp. 240-46.

in sharp decline, they organized themselves at the height of the internecine African conflict as the Casablanca bloc powers and supported a Pan-African movement against the so-called Monrovia powers which, in varying degrees, endorsed Eurafricanism. Then to the discredit of their own thesis, however, the opponents of Eurafricanism turned to other outsiders for their support. Deriving directly out of the Eurafrican problem, in effect, Africa thereupon became one of the most bitterly contested areas of the Cold War.

Without going into the details of Pan-African objections to association with the Eurafrican community [10] one can conveniently group them in two categories for a very brief examination. In essence, they are that the Eurafrican association is a violation of African neutralism in the East-West struggle, and second, that it constitutes neocolonialism.

Bitterly opposed by the Communist world, for example, the European Common Market according to the Pan-Africanists, is obviously a weapon in the Cold War. Association with the EEC, therefore, makes one a participant in the East-West struggle and thus violates two cardinal principles of Pan-African international politics. For literally conceptualizing themselves politically, as well as economically, as part of a so-called *tiers monde*, Pan-Africanists have assumed not only an allegedly neutral posture but also a role as "Third Force" between East and West. A neatly combined phrase, Egyptian "positive neutralism," is supposed to express both aspects of the posture.[11]

An important element of the Pan-African movement, the All African Trade Union Federation (AATUF) embraces the labor movements of the old Casablanca bloc powers, plus some others. Placing its orientation in clear perspective, it demanded at its founding congress in Casablanca in May, 1961, that African

---

[10]See McKay, *op. cit.*; Arnold Rivkin, *Africa and the West: Elements of Free-World Policy* (New York: Praeger, 1962), and his *Africa and the European Common Market: A Perspective*, Monograph No. 2--1963-64, University of Denver Monograph Series in World Affairs (Denver: University of Denver, 1964).

[11]See Simon Jargy, "Du neutralisme positif au non-alignement," *Orient*, Vol. V, No. 1 (2e trimestre 1961), pp. 15-22; and Fayez A. Sayegh (ed.), *The Dynamics of Neutralism in the Arab World: A Symposium* (San Francisco: Chandler Publishing Co., 1964).

labor movements disaffiliate with the International Confederation of Free Trade Unions (ICFTU) on the grounds that the Europeans and Americans dominate it. And, of course, out of the sheer weight of their numbers and resources, they do indeed dominate the ICFTU, despite their attempts at ameliorating the unfavorable balance that Africans and affiliates from other underdeveloped areas face within it.

AATUF also opposed, from its inception, African association with the Common Market. Adopted at the founding congress, this orientation has been maintained to the present.[12]

> Economic and financial ties with the West are still strong, not to mention the Western political, military and ideological influence that is deeply rooted in most African regions. African people have to beware of this plight and be always on the alert....
>
> Those anti-nationalists from among the Africans-- and thank God they are not many--are endeavoring hard to win for the Western line more African states through associating them with the Common Market ....
>
> All these forces are cooperating to help ex-imperialist empires come in through doors after they were thrown out of windows.

Embracing both economic and political objections to the Eurafrican community, Pan-African charges of neocolonialism summarize all the objections to association with the Common Market. Allegedly weighted heavily in Europe's favor, Eurafricanism will serve Europe at Africa's expense. In other words, Eurafricanism is essentially European rather than African. Pan-Africanism is an African concept, on the other hand, that in theory at least should unite Africa and its enormous natural and human resources and make it a world power. Focusing on Africa's raw statistics--a population, for example,

---

[12]"Neo-Colonialism and Africa," *The African Worker* (April, 1965), Monthly Bulletin published by the International Confederation of Arab Trade Unions, Cairo. See also the AATUF Charter of 1961 and the Complete Charter approved at the Second AATUF Congress convened in Bamako in June, 1964.

roughly equivalent to Western Europe's, and enormous reserves of natural resources--one must agree that this is a valid conclusion, provided the development process is given time.

EUROPE: MEETING THE CHALLENGE?

Stated in its simplest terms, the African associates of the European Common Market receive tariff preferences for their products in the European market in return for reduced tariffs on exports of the European Six into the associated African countries. Tariffs are to be gradually reduced. The Treaty of Rome foresaw a gradual elimination of the subsidies that the colonial powers, particularly France, provided to certain African crops. The European Six as a whole, however, have seen fit to continue certain of the subsidies, at least for the time being.

Observing Eurafricanism in this framework, the Pan-Africanists still charged neocolonialism. They stated that the system is obviously weighted to preserve the status quo between the developed Six and the underdeveloped associated African states. As a by-product of their association with the EEC, for example, the African states will have freer trade with each other by virtue of generally reduced tariffs within the EEC. Since the lines of each also run to Europe, however, large-scale indigenous industrial development in Africa allegedly is unlikely to occur despite increased intra-African trade.

Allowing the associated African states to levy tariffs within the EEC framework to protect their new industries, however, the Treaty of Rome provided an apparent rebuttal to the charge. Also offsetting allegations of this sort in another way, the Treaty of Rome instituted the European Fund for the Overseas Countries and Territories. The sum of $581.25 million was allocated to the Fund for economic and social development for five years, 1958-62. Renewed under the new Convention of Association of 1963, the Fund allocated $800 million for the next five years, almost all of which was again designated for Africa.

Nevertheless, it is of interest that the funds allocated to economic sectors have been designed to augment Eurafrican trade in its present form. Discounting those funds set apart for the social sectors, for example, one notes that those allocated for economic sectors embrace transportation, communications, agriculture and animal breeding. Thus, while the present Eurafrican relationship does not preclude the possibility of evolution in the pattern of products exchanged between Europe and Africa, it is definitely oriented toward maintaining it.

Very explicit on this point, AATUF has denounced the extension of the Common Market to Africa as an insidious form of colonialism:[13]

> The most dangerous thing about this form of colonialism is that it is without arms or occupation; its objective is to maintain its mastery over the region to get raw materials, agricultural products, and food stuffs at paltry prices. To this effect, the West has used versatile means and ways explicitly showing aid, sympathy and a will to develop Africa but implicitly carrying the destruction of the continent with it....

The crux of the Eurafrican issue, as far as the Pan-African opposition is concerned, has been precisely this point, that is, African development. For within the framework of their relations with the EEC, they feel that they are disadvantaged in terms of African development. No one can argue, for example, that the shipping of crude oil to Europe from Libya or Algeria is as advantageous to the producing countries as processing the crude first before it is exported. In effect, serious African critics of the EEC are interested in industrial development to process their own products prior to export; thus, they are not isolationists *per se*. Extremists among the African opposition to Eurafricanism, on the other hand, argue that Africa must first be left alone to develop itself. They are, of course, isolationists.

Although it is denied, the Pan-African labor movement AATUF falls within the latter category. Objecting to the ex-

---

[13]*Idem.*, (April, 1965).

treme isolationism of AATUF, on the other hand, 40 labor movements representing 30 African states established the African Trade Union Confederation (ATUC) in January, 1962. Reflecting the multilateral orientation of the former Monrovia powers (whose labor movements constitute the core of the organization), ATUC opposes the orientation of the Casablanca bloc powers that AATUF embodies. Unlike AATUF, for example, ATUC allows its affiliates to retain their membership in the ICFTU. Moreover, it does not oppose African association with the European Common Market.

From the European point of view, Africa is at this point a logical supplier of food and raw materials rather than industrial or manufactured products. In effect, Africa must be realistic about its stage of development. That trade between two areas automatically implies subordination of the one to the other, of course, is also denounced as nonsense. Indeed, proponents of Eurafricanism note that increasing African trade with Europe would help resolve Africa's balance of payments and provide funds for the very industrial development Africa wants.

Nevertheless, Pan-African labor leaders fear that Europe's increasing dependence on African products will force it to seek assurances, first by encouragement and, if that fails, by force, that the African supply of the products continues. Like the Middle East, which thought that its oil would bring independence from Europe, Africa too will find itself bound more closely than ever to Europe in a vital, but secondary role. Its economic--and political--systems will become inextricably subordinated to European interests. At least these are the fears of the Pan-Africanists.

There is some basis in fact for their fears. For as the EEC itself has noted, financial aid has already been a disappointing failure: A study of 37 underdeveloped states revealed that they are moving into unsupportable indebtedness.[14] Recalling similar situations in the history of the Ottoman Empire, of Egypt in the nineteenth century, and elsewhere, one could conceivably visualize the price Africa may also pay someday. Europeans could well be back to see that the African countries are properly run so that they can both service their debts and

---

[14]See *Problèmes Africains*, No. 296 (August 5, 1965).

keep up production of the raw materials and food which Europe needs. To counter this very real possibility, in fact, the European Fund of the EEC has allocated most of its funds as non-repayable grants.

PAN-AFRICAN FRUSTRATION AND FAILURES

Attracting far more attention than Eurafricanism which in large measure indeed generated it, Pan-Africanism has advocated an Africa for the Africans; in effect, the very antithesis of the Eurafrican community. As the leading protagonists of Pan-Africanism, President Sekou Touré of Guinea and former President of Ghana, Kwame Nkrumah, argued that the European Common Market is a sinister neocolonial vehicle. Under its cover, Europe will continue to exploit Africa as a source of cheap raw materials and then, in turn, as a closed market for the manufactured product.

Opposing association with the European Common Market as both complicity in the East-West struggle and as neocolonialism, therefore, the Pan-Africanists have advocated the creation of an African common market in lieu of association with the EEC. Arguing that the EEC is an exploitative device, Pan-Africanists suggest that Africans should themselves exploit their own resources. Allegedly possessing complementary products, the African states constitute a naturally self-sufficient community.

Merely a cursory check of the exports of a random handful of African states within reasonable geographical proximity to each other for easy commerce, however, reveals both the frustration of the Pan-Africanists and the validity of some sort of Eurafrican relationship, at least at this point (See Table 16, page 187).

Established in 1963 under the auspices of the United Nations, the African Development Bank enlisted the endorsement of 22 African states. The African common market, on the other hand, has not yet been realized and its prospects are dim. Openly critical of the concept, in fact, Tunisian President Bourguiba and Senegalese President Senghor, among others, have written it off as impracticable.[15] But Pan-Africanist as well as Pan-Maghrebist Algerian President Ben Bella provided an excellent practical example of both the intra- and inter-regional problems that an African common market must face.

TABLE 16
Exports of Selected African States

Country	Major Exports	Country	Major Exports
Senegal	Groundnuts	Dahomey	Palm kernels
Nigeria	Groundnuts		Palm oil
Mauretania	Iron ore	Libya	Petroleum
Ivory Coast	Coffee	Morocco	Phosphates
	Cocoa		Oranges
	Wood		Manganese
Togo	Cocoa	Tunisia	Phosphates
	Coffee		Iron
	Cotton		Lead
	Palm nuts		Wheat
	Phosphates		Olive oil
			Wine
		Algeria	Petroleum
			Wine

Source: *International Financial Statistics,* Vol. XVIII, Nos. 1-12, *passim.*

---

[15] See Bourguiba's comments in the official party organ *L'Action,* summarized in the *Maghreb Digest,* Vol. I, No. 12 (December, 1963), p. 43; *ibid.,* Vol. II, No. 2 (January, 1964), p. 32; and Léopold Senghor, *loc. cit.*

[16] For an elaboration of relations between North and sub-Saharan Africa, see Willard A. Beling, "North African Vision of Black Africa: Social and Economic Aspects," *Maghreb Digest,* Vol. IV, No. 1 (January, 1966), pp. 6-17.

Entitled to automatic association with the EEC as a member of the Franco-African community, Guinea had, in effect, rejected both in the referendum on the new French Constitution in 1958. As a former British colony, on the other hand, Ghana, at least initially, was less involved directly with EEC than Guinea. Nevertheless, Dr. Nkrumah was, if anything, more truculently hostile to the EEC than Sekou Touré. Less antagonistic to Western associations for some time than Ghana, Guinea nevertheless continues to oppose African association with the European Common Market. The removal of Dr. Nkrumah as President of Ghana, of course, makes Ghana's future relations with the EEC a moot question. Enjoying a competitive advantage over Ghana in exporting cocoa, however, Nigeria's proposed association with the European Common Market will undoubtedly influence the decision of Ghana, which is also a major cocoa exporter.[17]

Mistakenly discounted at times as non-African, the Arab states of the Maghreb (North Africa) have sometimes behaved more as Africans than as Arabs. Emphasizing African ties at the apparent expense of Pan-Arabism, for example, the Moroccan constitution of 1962 revealed a syndrome that has been relatively common in the Maghreb for the past several years. Besides Mali, Guinea and Ghana, for example, the well-known Pan-African grouping known as the Casablanca bloc powers also included Algeria and, of course, Morocco. While it did not embrace Tunisia or Libya, both have participated in a number of African conferences and, in fact, the former has hosted several of them.

Although excluded from North Africa as a subregion, Egypt as part of "Northern" Africa has also closely identified itself with Africa and the Pan-African position. The second circle of Nasser's *Philosophy of the Revolution* had, in effect, clearly identified Egypt with Africa, as well as with the Arab and Islamic worlds. The subsequent Egyptian involvement in the Congo affair, among others, demonstrated the practical implications. Egypt was, of course, an important element in the Casablanca bloc powers.

---

[17]Although Ghana has apparently sold a large part of its cocoa production of this year and perhaps next to the U.S.S.R., the terms may well have been to Ghana's disadvantage.

There is an apparent conflict of interests between Pan-Arabism, of which Egypt is the obvious leader, and Pan-Africanism, since each advocates its own common market. Preoccupied with its own regional defense system, however, Egypt views Africa essentially as a vital ancillary in terms of the Arab-Israeli conflict. Limited by the Arab boycott and the Arab *cordon sanitaire*, for example, Israel's trade union has been essentially with Europe rather than Africa, although it is cultivating the African market assiduously. Recognizing that EEC association is almost a matter of life or death for Israel, naturally Egypt hopes that she will not win it. But Africa is also involved. Common Israeli and African association with the EEC would undo, in effect, the Arab boycott that Egypt has sought to establish in Africa against Israel.[18]

Although the United Arab Republic remains opposed to the Common Market, it is noteworthy that its other erstwhile Arab allies in the Casablanca bloc powers have, in the meantime, been seeking to negotiate association with the EEC. Under the formula that *Algerie est française*, Algeria was brought automatically into the Common Market, although its exact status in practice remained unclear. That the revolutionary Provisional Government of the Republic of Algeria was then part of the Casablanca bloc powers, of course, had nothing to do with the relationship of Algeria with the Common Market at this point. In the meantime,

---

[18]See R. K. Ramazani, *The Middle East and the European Common Market* (Charlottesville: University Press of Virginia, 1964). It is interesting to note that AATUF identifies Israel and its labor movement, the Histadrut, as part of the neocolonial plot in Africa. Meeting in Accra on February 10-13, 1965, for example, the AATUF Executive Committee resolved that there is an "absolute necessity for the peoples of Africa to pursue and intensify their just struggle against international imperialism, colonialism, neo-colonialism, Zionism as well as feudalism and other reactionary tendencies...." *The African Worker*, op. cit. (March, 1965). A founding member of AATUF, the Egyptian labor movement has assumed the same concern over the Palestine issue within the Pan-African labor movement as the Egyptian Government has in other African groupings. Like Pan-Africanism itself when set within its proper framework, the Egyptian position is also understandable--even if not universally appreciated--when it is removed from the Cold War context in which it is usually placed and is considered within the framework of its own defense system.

however, independent Algeria has been negotiating for association with the EEC in spite of the uncompromising Algerian posture on colonialism. Another Maghrebi partner in the Casablanca grouping, Morocco, has also been engaged in negotiations with the Common Market.[19]

Openly aided and abetted by the Soviets and Red Chinese, Ghana and Guinea have been justifiably suspect as being inspired by more than Pan-African idealism. In recent years, therefore, the activities of both have become almost as offensive to most Africans as they have been to non-Africans. Endorsing in effect the Monrovia powers' position, however, the 1963 Addis Ababa Conference of Heads of State and Government dealt a serious blow to their position.

Yet there are other African states that one cannot label as participants in the Guinea-Ghanaian form of Pan-Africanism, or as dupes of international Communism; they have also opposed the Eurafrican concept. The former British colonies, for example, had initially opposed almost *en masse* African association with the Common Market. Precluded in effect by definition until 1963 from association, of course, they drew some comfort in their opposition to the EEC in the fact that Ghana and Guinea could not label them as imperialist lackeys on this score. As noted earlier, however, when it was thrown open to them, they reversed their stand in favor of association with the EEC. On the other hand, Ethiopia, the Sudan and Liberia have expressed no particular interest one way or the other regarding the Common Market.

Pan-Africanism has failed, in effect, on both defense and offense. Unable to block African association with the European Common Market, it has also failed to establish viable Pan-African alternatives. Even what was considered its most basic Pan-African organization, the Pan-African labor movement, has fallen on hard times. Enduring a serious setback when AFRO was created in 1960--while AATUF was established later, in 1961, it had been envisaged considerably earlier--it suffered a disastrous defeat when ATUC was established in 1962. In

---

[19]Mali, the only other member of the Casablanca grouping not discussed, had been associated, ironically, with the EEC from the inception.

effect, the creation of ATUC undid any chances for an all-embracing continental Pan-African labor movement.

This does not imply, of course, that ATUC is a success. It also arose, in fact, in large measure out of tacit dissatisfaction with the ICFTU and quite obviously with its African Regional Organization (AFRO), to which many of ATUC's Affiliates belonged. Dissatisfied with AFRO, in any case, its African affiliates created the African Trade Union Confederation in 1962. Obviously a redundancy, it appears to have been an attempt to create what they felt was an acceptable African alternative to AFRO itself. In the face of both these expressions of African labor dissatisfaction, the ICFTU African Regional Organization has not developed. All three of these African labor organizations, in fact, are essentially moribund.

It is of interest to note that under the leadership of its Moroccan President, Mahjoub Ben Seddik, AATUF remains formally adamant in its opposition to Eurafricanism. Its opposition, however, has become a very tenuous thing. For in the meantime, even Ben Seddik's government has reversed its position on Pan-Africanism's hard line vis-à-vis Europe, which it had endorsed as a member of the Casablanca powers. The Algerian Government has also reversed itself; both it and Morocco have applied for associational membership in the European Common Market. In the Algerian case, of course, this is important, since the Algerian Government controls the Algerian labor movement.

More recently, the Ghanaian position has also become doubtful. The Ghanaian Trades Union Congress had assumed a paramount position in AATUF in 1964. Following the recent military takeover, however, they appear destined to relinquish it again to the *Union Marocaine du Travail*. It is even possible that the Ghanaian TUC may eventually withdraw from AATUF. In summary, AATUF opposition to Eurafricanism is considerably weaker today than the number of its affiliated movements implies.

VIABLE ALTERNATIVES TO EURAFRICANISM?

That some African states have rejected the Eurafrican

concept altogether need not imply that they are better off than the others. Their subordination to some other extra-African group may indeed be fraught with more danger than they assume is implicit in Eurafricanism. Guinea and Ghana are good cases in point regarding both their internal affairs and their Pan-African aspirations. Foundering in economic shambles, for example, both have had to make serious adjustments; indeed, Ghanaian President Nkrumah has been ousted. Also under their aegis, the Pan-African AATUF was often subjected to manipulation by the Soviet-dominated World Federation of Trade Unions, to the undoing of the appeal that the Pan-African labor movement might have had in many African states.

On the other hand, when the African associates of the EEC formally rejected the term "Eurafrican Community" as objectionable, they did not thereby undo the paramount position that Europe occupies in the relationship. For within the present Eurafrican frame of reference, relations between sovereign African and European states are perforce balanced in Europe's favor. It can dictate the terms of the Eurafrican relationship.

Deriving from a long-enduring pique, for example, President Charles de Gaulle has refused Tunisian overtures for closer relations. Unrealistic? Of course not. Tunisia needs France; France does not need Tunisia. In vain, therefore, President Bourguiba has gone almost as far as the head of a sovereign state perhaps can to rebuild Franco-Tunisian ties without going all the way to Canossa. On the other hand, Algeria has fared better than its neighbor because France needs its oil. Indeed, Algerian fresh fruits and vegetables have moved into the European Common Market even though Algeria is not an associate. (The export of fruits and vegetables to the EEC has been one of the important issues that has been a stumbling block in the negotiations of the other Maghreb states for association with the European Common Market.)

Facing the loss of their traditional share of the European market to other states that have already associated with the EEC, the hard-pressed African states tend to choose association with the Common Market rather than continue to fight it. In reality there is no comparable alternative to which they can turn. The implications of preferential treatment of Algerian oil in the Common Market, for example, may well force similar considerations in the Middle East. Europe is, of course, their biggest customer. Facing further the fact that they are not sharing in the European Fund, of course, other hesitant African states are now giving serious consideration to joining the Eurafrican community.

RELATIONS OUTSIDE THE EURAFRICAN FRAMEWORK

The evolving American role in the Eurafrican issue is of particular interest. Committed to European recovery and its ability to stand against the Communist threat, for example, the United States had encouraged European cooperation and integration. The Organization for European Economic Cooperation (OEEC), therefore, was established as a first step in 1948 to coordinate American aid that was to pour into war-devastated Europe under the Marshall Plan. That the colonial ties between Europe and its overseas territories should be reflected in OEEC, of course, was completely logical at this point. Deriving out of the earlier OEEC, the European Economic Community in turn retained the ties with the overseas territories, even though they were now free or were destined soon to be independent.

Exercised subsequently over the Communist threat to Africa, the United States also appeared on balance to favor the concept of a Eurafrican community as defined in the Treaty of Rome. The United States obviously preferred it to the only apparent alternative at the time, the Pan-African community which, under Ghanaian and Guinean leadership, protested non-alignment but in fact had dealings with international Communism. Nevertheless, the United States had had no real choice in the matter. For Eurafricanism had been essentially a unilateral European concept which, indeed, had been in large measure a French decision, initially.

Excluded by definition from the European Economic Community, the United States has protested against EEC exclusiveness and more recently against its extension to the Eurafrican community. Charging that the tariff walls being erected around the Eurafrican community within the EEC framework are contrary to GATT agreements, for example, the United States has clearly pointed up the issue.

American protests against the European Six's position in Africa--EEC negotiations, for example, with Nigeria--derive from a relatively recent development. For as long as the Eurafrican community had been limited essentially to the francophonic states, tariff walls had not really been a point of issue. They had retained close ties with the former metropole since their independence. Now that EEC appeared on the threshold of embracing other African states that had, since their independence, developed ties with the United States, however, the issue was certain to be drawn. Nigeria, of course, is a good case in point.

Objecting to an exclusive European community, the United States is also opposed to a resurgence of exclusive European relations with Africa. Perhaps overstated when labeled neocolonialism, exclusive European ties with Africa are allegedly objectionable, if merely for Africa's sake. Opposed thus to the European Six in Africa, the position of the United States obviously corresponds, to a degree at least, with that of the less extreme elements of Pan-Africanism and certainly, of course, with the multilateral concept of the former Monrovia powers. With these parameters, therefore, one can expect pressures to mount in Africa against European predominance in the Eurafrican community.

Excluded by definition from the Eurafrican community, however, the United States is essentially an outsider. Thus, the Africans themselves must in effect improve their own positions vis-à-vis Europe in the Eurafrican community. It may take time. Only when the Algerians forced the issue, for example, did they win concessions in their oil agreement with France that imply industrialization and their participation in the process. Since then they seem to relate well with Europe.

As for relations with African labor, the American labor movement had joined forces with them on a similar issue as early as the Third ICFTU World Congress held in Stockholm in 1953. Through their combined efforts they were able to correct the balance of power in the ICFTU which had been heavily weighted in favor of the Europeans. In the meantime, the American labor movement has taken further steps to thwart the overriding European influence still remaining in the ICFTU.

While still a part of the International Confederation of Free Trade Unions, for example, American labor has moved increasingly into independent activities in Africa. The recently established African-American Labor Center is a case in point. The conflict of interests between the American and European labor movements, of course, was also revealed in the establishment of the African Trade Union Confederation. For it was apparent that it enjoyed American labor's sympathy, if indeed not its support, at the expense of the ICFTU-sponsored African Regional Organization (AFRO).

Within this context, therefore, it is reasonable to assume that a rapprochement could also take place between the American labor movement and the adamant African labor opposition to Eurafricanism, all other things being equal. Indeed, there is evidence that this is already occurring.

CONCLUSION

In conclusion, Eurafricanism has already prevailed at the expense of Pan-Africanism. Whether this discredits African objections entirely, however, is another matter. In the extreme form of Pan-African xenophobic opposition, yes, but not entirely in other forms of opposition. For like the Europeans who objected to the mismatch that is implicit in a closely knit Atlantic community, serious Africans retain their misgivings regarding a closely integrated Eurafrican community. But unlike the loosely tied Atlantic community, a rather inflexibly implemented Eurafricanism has emerged.

While not tantamount perhaps to neocolonialism, Eurafricanism obviously carries implications that are at least as serious as those which a much more politically and economically developed Europe had found intolerable in a closely knit Atlantic community. They appear more serious, in fact, because the mismatch between Europe and Africa is even more obvious. Allowing no viable alternative that is readily apparent to the Africans, therefore, unilaterally restrictive economic Eurafricanism will certainly continue to generate political frustrations which will spill over into the international arena.

Although rebuffed in Africa for the most part, international

Communism will continue to exploit the situation. On the other hand, those of the West who are excluded by definition will also object to the exclusive Eurafrican club, if merely on grounds that it is against African interests. American labor's involvement in Africa seems to fall in large measure within this framework. Others have also begun to take sides on the implications of Eurafricanism. Ironically, the hitherto much-maligned Pan-African response to Eurafricanism is becoming more respectable.

CHAPTER **10** LABOR: THE PROBLEM OF INTERNATIONAL DIALOGUE

Donald C. Bergus [†]

Nongovernmental dialogue between differing countries and peoples is not only a good thing but an essential element in modern diplomacy. There are so-called purists who hold to the traditional view that relations between nations are *ipso facto* relations between governments. The traditionalist believes that if there should be a dialogue between nations, it should be conducted exclusively according to the rules of the Congress of Vienna and at the stately tempo and according to the classic forms established in the nineteenth century. But those who believe that only appropriately commissioned bureaucrats have the mission of speaking with foreigners, that all others who go abroad should confine themselves to the role of tourist, teacher, or businessman, have long been discredited. Even the forms of traditional diplomacy have largely been discarded except by a few.

Certainly since the end of World War I, it has been generally recognized that international dialogue between associational groups is not only a useful supplement to traditional diplomacy but an absolutely necessary element of modern relations between states. There is little to commend a situation where the only meaningful conversations which take place between two countries are those going on between the officialdom of both sides. The only way to describe such relations is very

---

[†]Donald C. Bergus has been a Foreign Service Officer since 1942; Counselor of Embassy for Political Affairs, Cairo (1962-1965); and U.S. Department of State Senior Fellow in the School of International Relations, University of Southern California (1965-1966).

thin and narrow.

THE DIALOGUE WITHIN THE ATLANTIC COMMUNITY

It figures among the national objectives to broaden or thicken the relations between states. Consider, for example, American relations with Britain. Here is a case where in the last century, scholars, statesmen, trade unionists, businessmen, and many others have built up such a thickly woven cable between the two countries that relations between the two governments, while an important number of strings in this cable, are only part of the whole. It is probably true that prior to America's entry into World War II, the American people as a whole were ahead of their government in the conviction that what Britain stood for should not be destroyed by the Nazi onslaught. Observers of events during the Suez crisis of 1956 have testified that had there not been this broad skein of relations between all sorts of groups in the two countries, the trauma which arose in the official relations between the two governments would have taken a much longer time to heal.

Consider American relations with France. It is probably no exaggeration to state that official relations with America's oldest ally have not been easy or comfortable since France fell in 1940. Certain it is that the United States disagreed with the French about Southeast Asia ever since the end of World War II. It is equally certain that there are few world problems which the United States Government and the present Government of France can agree about. But neither side is ready to cast the other into outer darkness. There is too much in common between the two peoples.

THE DIALOGUE WITH THE DEVELOPING AREAS

Here we are primarily concerned with the developing countries. But when one searches for examples where there is this breadth of relationships among peoples, where a genuine dialogue at the international level between associational interest groups is taking place, such examples are, alas, too few. In fact, the dialoguers may be losing ground. Take India and the United States, for example. Whether the broad understandings that existed, despite serious governmental differences, between Americans and peoples and interest groups in India will survive the demise of Nehru is not yet established.

But the dialogue between American associational interest groups and their counterparts abroad can be crucial at times. After the Lebanon crisis of 1958, after President Nasser had decided on the Soviet Union as his sole supplier of vast quantities of weapons, after the Soviets had taken on the task of assisting Egypt in building the High Dam on the Nile, official relations between the Egyptian Government and the United States were virtually nonexistent. It is interesting that for a period the only mutual enthusiasm shared by Americans and Egyptians was among the groups of archeologists of both countries. Everybody could agree as to the necessity of saving the temples of Nubia and Abu Simbel from the Nile flood. A dialogue was established which set the stage for the United States and Egypt to re-establish a relationship which, while still subject to periodic crisis, was reasonably acceptable and mutually beneficial.

Thus far, an effort has been made to establish two things. One, that a genuine dialogue between all sorts of associational interest groups is a vital part of present-day international relations. Two, that Western groups have yet to establish such a dialogue with the vast majority of underdeveloped countries. Let us pose a few problems which labor faces in establishing a dialogue in underdeveloped countries.

A meaningful and effective dialogue between the American labor movement, for example, and its counterparts in the developing countries has not yet been established. This, despite the fact that American unions and labor specialists in the American Government have put much by way of resources and personnel into the effort. If anything, their good will, their good intentions, have outrun their accomplishment. Perhaps they have mistaken investment and assignment of personnel for achievement.

American labor and the government have been less quick to realize that something should be done in this field. But the results have yet to be impressive. Until one examines some fundamentals, one sees no early improvement in this situation. Agreed that organized labor is important as a link among peoples, one has little at this stage to demonstrate except men in motion, or people in commotion, as the fruition of all the efforts.

The magnitude and generosity of American labor's efforts in arranging and financing exchange visits, training activities and other endeavors to build cooperation with the labor leadership of developing countries is impressive. But much of this activity remains peripheral.

As for government, one gets the impression that the Departments of State and Labor have more people constantly pointing out how important labor is than they have those prepared to give thought to the essence of the problem. It would be better if some of these people devoted some of their time to thinking through some of the basic problems which prevent the establishment of more meaningful dialogue with labor leaders in developing countries.

Most of the problems which arise come from fundamental differences in national development, particularly in the Near East and Africa since 1960. It is only by recognizing such differences that one can make progress in resolving them.

IDEOLOGICAL FACTORS

Let us look at the ideological set of problems. Let us recognize that it was the trade union movement in the West which more than anything else gave the lie to the theories dreamed up by Karl Marx, grubbing away in the library of the British Museum, as to the pattern which the future should inexorably take. It is thanks to trade unionism that Marx's description of capitalism as he saw it in England in the middle of the nineteenth century has become hopelessly outdated. Let us also recognize, that in the immediate postwar struggle, the period of the Marshall Plan in Europe, American labor had a genuine interest in preventing European unions from translating their legitimate grievances into active Communism. Surely this battle has been largely won, but apparently the United States has kept on some of the same ideas (and some of the same idea men) from that battle to cope with the present task of developing a useful dialogue with the labor leaders of the developing states. There is no question that the issue of the future mission of the ICFTU in the developing countries is a very live one among free world trade union leaders. But still there is much to be said for proclaiming a moratorium on ideology in dialogue with trade unionists in the developing countries for a while. With a few notable exceptions, in most of the developing countries, what local capital is raised for development will come from governmental measures. While generally, this process is more akin to statism--the étatism of Mustafa Kemal's Turkey of the 1920's--one must brace himself for public declarations that governments and unions have adopted the purest form of socialism and that they recognize the USSR as a useful source of socialist ideas.

One can argue that it would be preferable to note such remarks and pass on to meaningful work rather than to involve ourselves in lengthy ideological discussions. The doctrine of leftward-leaning "nonalignment," the acceptance of something called socialism is too deeply ingrained in most developing countries. Surely it behooves one to relegate these proclamations to their proper place for a while, to avoid seeking signatures on petitions, and, in the words of Voltaire, "to cultivate our garden."

If the Near East is any example, there are three countries where Soviet theories have had more than a fair trial-- Egypt, Syria and Iraq. But very probably none of the three will end up with a system that could really be identified with the Soviet system.

SOCIOLOGICAL AND ECONOMIC FACTORS

The next group of problems is sociological. The American labor movement has been eminently successful in bringing about a situation whereby highly skilled workers earn what they deserve. The United States accepts not only the principle of the dignity of labor but the fact that each should reap something roughly commensurate with his contribution to the society and the economy. There is hardly a developing country where this principle has been accepted. In too many developing societies, status counts more than contribution. The smallest pencil pusher in the government bureau has more social worth than the most skilled and highly trained worker. In such societies leadership of the trade union movement sometimes becomes important as an escape from the stigma of being a worker, rather than for its task of active defense of the worker's rights.

This problem becomes most serious when a society fails or lags in developing personnel at the foreman level in industrial enterprises. But there is no answer to the problem. It is not certain that the history alone of what the American movement has done in this regard is in itself applicable to countries such as Upper Volta or Algeria. Of course, this problem is under extensive study. Nevertheless, it needs increased attention.

The next series of problems, the economic, is even more difficult. Let us return to the basic assumption that in most developing countries capital for new enterprises almost always comes from the state. But to this mix one must add extreme nationalism, itself a rather healthy manifestation from our point of view. But the problems it creates are highly complex. The following is an extreme example.

In Egypt there is an automobile assembly plant owned and financed by the government. It purchases assemblies, with scarce hard currency, from the Fiat complex in Italy. The market for the product, which is sold for the local soft currency, is insatiable. The labor force of the plant, fixed by government and the local unions, is about 6,000. These workers report for duty and draw their pay regardless of production schedules. Sometimes, when the Cairo authorities are flush, they turn out a respectable number of units. Other times, when foreign exchange is tight, and these times are the most frequent, they still come to work and draw their pay. There have been days when all 6,000 workers have turned out about 20 units. Each of those little Fiats (although called Nasr, or Victory, cars in Egypt) probably costs the Egyptian taxpayer more than an imported Cadillac. In a broad diversified economy, this situation would, in time, right itself. But in Egypt, where the alternatives are so few, one might be witnessing the establishment of a new industrial peonage.

This problem exists in one form or another in various developing countries. Part of the answer may lie in giving organized labor a voice in the development process which goes beyond present pressures but involves a responsibility for valid economic growth.

POLITICAL FACTORS

The final set of problems has to do with politics. The role that organized labor played in most developing countries in assuring the success of national revolutions for independence has been noteworthy. There are few newly independent countries which do not count several trade union leaders among their national heroes. But once that independence is achieved, it too often becomes another story. In the resulting statist society, the professional trade unionist is either neutralized or willingly becomes a servant of the state, a mere "transmission belt."

To return to the Near East again, the one or two Arab countries where the labor movement bears the most resemblance to Western unions are the countries where something akin to what we call "free enterprise" has been adopted--primarily for reasons having nothing to do with economics or ideology. These are Lebanon and Jordan. But look at Egypt. In 1954, when Nasser was fighting not only for ascendancy in the government but for his very survival, it was the streetcar workers' union that saw him through the most difficult period.

But once the political objectives are gained, too often and too willingly the unions with their leadership sink into the position of becoming the *agitprop*, the organizable spontaneous demonstrators, on behalf of the regime. This is deplorable because in developing countries, unions can and must furnish future national leadership. But from all indications this is not going to happen. Here again is something worth intensive study.

One final thought: Labor must broaden its capabilities to face up to difficult international issues. One of the most difficult, one of the hardiest perennials in today's world is the unresolved Arab-Israeli conflict. Many American unions and their leaders, for example, are fully committed to the independence and integrity of the state of Israel. Many Arab labor leaders, either by conviction or direction, proclaim the destruction of that state as a national and social goal. Surely American labor has to be a little more realistic in assessing this issue in terms of its relations with the Arab, North African, and some of the African states.

CONCLUSION

In summary, a valid dialogue does not exist between the labor movements of the developed and the developing countries. The lack of such a dialogue comes not from a lack of mutual effort and desire, but from a lack of substance and concern. Both substance and concern, however, may be achieved with more effort.

Labor has a fascinating challenge in its future dialogue with its counterparts in the developing areas. It has a unique role to play in working with hundreds of millions of people for a better future.